Devotions Day by Day

From *The Secret Place*

Edited by *Phyllis A. Frantz*

Judson Press® Valley Forge

The devotions in this book first appeared in the 1980, 1981, 1982, 1983, 1984, 1985, 1986, and 1987 issues of *Secret Place,* edited by Vincie Alessi and Michael E. Dixon.

Copyright © 1988
Judson Press, Valley Forge, PA 19482-0851

Library of Congress Cataloging-in-Publication Data
Frantz, Phyllis A.
    Devotions day by day.

    1. Devotional calendars. I. Title.
BV4811.F73   1988   242'.2   88-848
ISBN 0-8170-1128-5

The name JUDSON PRESS is registered as a trademark in the U.S. Patent Office.
Printed in the U.S.A.

JANUARY

Hebrews 2:1–9   Contemplating the New Year

THOUGHT FOR TODAY: Therefore we ought to give the more earnest heed to the things which we have heard, lest at any time we should let them slip. Hebrews 2:1 (King James Version)

New Year's Day is not a holiday at our house. It is a work day—a day to put away all the "tinsel" of Christmas and restore the basic decor.

Frequently on this "put away" day the sun shines, and things that appeared by candlelight or tree light to be bright suddenly seem dull and unattractive, and I get the urge to clean, shine, and polish. When the cleaning is complete, many things seem to have a newness—a beauty that has been hidden.

As I work, I contemplate the New Year. I realize that if only I will let God's sunshine flood my life, I'll see spots that are tarnished.

The New Year will not bring miraculous changes for most of us. The miracle will come only as God gives us the vision and courage to take what we have and polish it for God.

PRAYER: Dear God, help us to keep our lives radiant. Rid us of dullness and help us in this New Year to be shining witnesses for you. For Jesus' sake, we pray. Amen.   *Ruth Shearer—Philippi, West Virginia*

4

Matthew 11:16–19   Come to the Crowd

THOUGHT FOR TODAY: "We piped to you, and you did not dance; we wailed, and you did not mourn." Matthew 11:17

The reference Jesus made about children's games reminds me of my childhood when a group of buddies armed with snowballs would shout to other boys and girls, "Come to the crowd." To refuse was to become a target for snowball ammunition.

Just as Jesus applied the ancient game/lesson to people who demanded participation in their funeral or wedding games, I wonder if we say, "Come to the crowd, or we will pelt you with snowballs of indifference, criticism, or sarcasm"?

Are we a "cold-shouldered" church or a warmhearted fellowship about which people say, "Behold, how they love one another"?

PRAYER: God, help us to bring people to "our crowd" by words and deeds of love and understanding. In Jesus' name. Amen.

Wayne A. Dalton—Sioux Falls, South Dakota

Isaiah 54:11–17   A Timeless Message

THOUGHT FOR TODAY: "Come unto me, all ye that labour and are heavy laden, and I will give you rest." Matthew 11:28 (King James Version)

When the new year started, I had a cold and virus that sapped all of my energy. I dragged myself to my full-time job almost every day, but work at home began to pile up around me. My disposition was beginning to match my health, and one day a family argument erupted over a minor incident.

Later I sat in the kitchen rearranging a box on the shelf. Inside I found some outdated items and started to discard them. One card had last year's calendar on it, and as I started to toss it into the waste can, I saw these words on the other side: "Come unto me, all ye that labour and are heavy laden, and I will give you rest."

The calendar had become outdated, but it carried a message that is as powerful today as it was the day it was first recorded.

PRAYER: Dear God, thank you for the timely words to my tired, aching body and my distressed mind. In Jesus' name. Amen.

Kathy Scott—Lancaster, Pennsylvania

5

Philippians 3:7–9   Jesus—Mine All the Time

THOUGHT FOR TODAY: Whatever the circumstances, let us not forget our reason for joy.

It was a gray and rainy day. As I neared the bus stop, my bus pulled away with a roar. I would have to wait for the next one. It began to rain harder. I was getting soaked to the skin and the frown on my face deepened as I thought of my misery. But then I thought of an old song I'd learned as an accompanist for a children's choir.

I had not much liked that job and had long ago written it off as an experience to be forgotten. But today I found myself beginning to smile as I hummed the chorus we'd learned there. "Why should I care if the sun doesn't shine? Jesus is mine, all of the time." I looked at myself and laughed. What difference should gray skies make when I knew Jesus? It was a wonderful day!

PRAYER: Jesus, thank you for the fleeting images and half-remembered thoughts that bring us back to focus on you. Amen.

Alan Carpenter—Minneapolis, Minnesota

1 Corinthians 3:13–16 · 100,000 Trees!

THOUGHT FOR TODAY: It is not because things are difficult that we do not dare; it is because we do not dare that they are difficult.

At eighty-eight years of age the old forester still stood well over six feet tall. He radiated grace and warmth with a quiet manner and ready smile. He was being interviewed for a small newsletter, and even though he was worn by the physical onslaught of his years, the questions brought easy responses. When he was in high school, he broke the track record for his state. When he was thirty-five, he was given a lifetime membership in the country club for his expertise in golf. He directed the forestry rehabilitation programs for five states during his career.

Then, when he was asked what was the single most significant thing he could pluck out of his eighty-eight years of living, he said simply, "I planted more than 100,000 trees." One hundred thousand trees! And in his eyes shone the lights of the universe.

PRAYER: Our great God, give us the will to dare those things you will then give us the strength to do. Amen.

Patricia Reasoner—Colchester, Vermont

6

Philippians 1:2–9 · Called By Name

THOUGHT FOR TODAY: . . . "I have called thee by thy name; thou art mine." Isaiah 43:1 (King James Version)

Rolf, a college student from West Germany, spent a weekend in our home while touring the United States. One Sunday morning we invited him to church.

Admitting that he was not a churchgoer, but perhaps thinking he would observe something different, he came along. The college group welcomed Rolf and asked him to come that evening for their meeting.

We were delighted that he was encouraged and drove him back to church. That evening after he came home he reported, "They prayed for me by name! I have *never* heard my name said in prayer before."

Rolf left the next day for the rest of his tour of the United States, and we lost contact with him; but I know he will never forget the night that someone spoke his name aloud in prayer before almighty God.

PRAYER: Oh, God, help us remember to bring to you the names of those who need you and have never met you. For Jesus' sake. Amen.

Mary Lou Klingler—Phoenix, Arizona

2 Corinthians 12:1–10   God's Grace

THOUGHT FOR TODAY: My grace is sufficient for thee: for my strength is made perfect in weakness. 2 Corinthians 12:9 (King James Version)

The painful effect of unemployment rippled through each area of his life, causing bankruptcy, marital stress, and poor self-image. I asked, "How do you counter the many negative forces in your life?" "I don't," he replied, "God does. Previously I knew God loved me, but I never had to live in that love. Now I must rely on God totally.

"My church," he continued, "has been tremendously supportive. They bought me that old Pinto to get to my new job. For two months we could not make house payments, and God's people helped. At Christmas there was absolutely no money to buy gifts for our nine-year-old son and four-year-old daughter. But the week before Christmas our driveway turned into Grand Central. God has flooded my life with goodness through the love of others."

PRAYER: God, thank you for opportunities you give us to serve you and for persons who respond in love. Amen.

Paul Aiello, Jr.—Southfield, Michigan

7

1 John 4:7–21   Love—Human and Divine

THOUGHT FOR TODAY: Beloved, if God so loved us, we ought also to love one another. 1 John 4:11

For many months I have watched two elderly ladies sitting together in the back pew of our church. They take care of each other in such a loving way. The younger, about eighty, can see a little better, so she always finds the right page in the hymnal. Then she carefully cleans her friend's glasses before they stand together and sing with gusto. After the service, with arms entwined, they help each other through the crowded narthex. My Sundays are blessed because of their presence.

How many of us care for our friends and families in such a loving manner? Do we lead them to sing God's praises? Do we help them to see God's will for their lives more clearly? Do we walk with them through the crowded, perhaps fearful, places of life?

PRAYER: Thank you, Lord, for teaching us that we must love one another before we can understand your love for us. Amen.

Carroll Sharpe—Santa Cruz, California

1 Samuel 16:1–7   Loving Makes Me Special

THOUGHT FOR TODAY: "Man looks at the outward appearance, but the LORD looks at the heart." 1 Samuel 16:7 (New International Version)

Not handsome, athletic, or popular, Joe didn't excel in the "antagonistic personality assets" (things a person excels in only when compared with others). Perched on a hunched back and a dwarfed body, his houndlike face peered at the world sadly. Like many of us, he daydreamed about having a body like a Greek god.

Then he got a job working with handicapped children. Identifying with their hurt, he worked to build up their self-esteem. With hugs and love, he'd say, "My, you run fast!" "What pretty brown eyes you have!" "You did great!" "You're a very special person!"

Despite their all-pervasive popular acceptance, the "heroic" qualities Joe lacked are a pathetic illusion. God's way says, "If you can show love, you can feel special."

PRAYER: God of love, teach me to feel special by making others feel special. For Jesus' sake. Amen.   *Luther Cross—Seaton, Illinois*

James 5:7–11   Dream Big Dreams

THOUGHT FOR TODAY: Brethren, do not be weary in well-doing. 2 Thessalonians 3:13

Nicholas was a half-hour late coming home from kindergarten. The roads were slippery with several inches of new snow. Worried mother Becky took the car and went to look for him. Halfway between school and home, she found her little boy struggling to push a huge snowball down the sidewalk.

"I was trying to bring a snowball home, Mom, but they keep getting so big I have to start over!" Nicholas's trail from the schoolhouse was punctuated with big, abandoned snowballs.

Was Nicholas dreaming too big a dream? Or had he simply learned the value of perseverance? God loves to take our failures and use them in ways we can't foresee—so let's keep on keeping on, even when our projects seem to end in failure.

PRAYER: Dear God, help me to remember when I am discouraged that you are making something beautiful out of my failures. Help me to persevere. Amen.   *Joan Biggar—Marysville, Washington*

2 Corinthians 12:7–10 The Thorn

THOUGHT FOR TODAY: . . . when I am weak, then I am strong—the less I have, the more I depend on him. (Based on 2 Corinthians 12:10, Good News Bible)

A hormonal imbalance was causing me to experience some uncomfortable and frightening physical reactions. Again and again I begged the Lord please to make me well, but I received no answer. I felt angry, hurt, and confused by his silence. And I kept asking, "Why?"

One day I was drawn to the above passage. Upon doing further research, I discovered that some biblical scholars believe Paul's "thorn" may have been epilepsy. What a devastating condition that would have been for early Christianity's greatest spokesman! More important than what Paul's thorn was, however, was what God was able to do in his life through it. When Paul finally stopped asking why, he received a miracle as great as healing—he discovered in a deeper way the adequacy and availability of God's resources.

PRAYER: Help us, Lord, to stop fighting our limitations in order that we might see in them the crown of blessing they can become. Amen.

Marlene J. Bagnull—Drexel Hill, Pennsylvania

9

Acts 1:1–8 Witnessing

THOUGHT FOR TODAY: ". . . You shall receive . . . and you shall be my witnesses. . . ." Acts 1:8

Did you ever hear of Boris Nicholayevich Kornfeld? He was a Russian medical doctor of Jewish ancestry. He incurred the displeasure of Stalin and was thrown into a *gulag*, where he became a believer in the Messiah. He did his best to practice medicine in a hopeless situation.

One gray afternoon Boris was attending a young prisoner who had just been operated on for cancer. Boris wanted to tell someone about his new life of obedience to Christ and freedom in Christ. All afternoon and late into the night the doctor described to his patient his conversion. The next morning, Boris Kornfeld was found dead from eight blows to the head, dealt by a vicious nocturnal intruder. The patient pondered the doctor's impassioned witness to his Savior, Jesus. The patient recovered. He too believed. He was released. His name? Alexandr Solzhenitzyn.

PRAYER: O Jesus, help me to witness to someone about you, even if it is only one, and under terrible circumstances. For your sake. Amen.

J. Lester Harnish—Lake Oswego, Oregon

Psalm 46   When Words Aren't Important

THOUGHT FOR TODAY: Sometimes we are so busy talking we forget the importance of listening.

You don't mind if I hold your hand?" he asked. Holding his cold hand reminded me of how terribly ill he was—and how young. Tears filled his eyes and his body shook from the force of his grief.

I asked God to give me some words which would help. After all, I *am* the pastor! I am the one who is expected to say the right thing. But the words just wouldn't come.

"Would you read to me from the Bible?" Soon I found myself reading: "Be still, and know that I am God" (Psalm 46:10).

We sat, hands clasped, in the stillness of the hospital room. God ministered—when words just weren't important!

PRAYER: Dear God, teach us the value of listening quietly for your still, small voice. In Jesus' name. Amen.

James O. Wolfe III—Salem, New Jersey

1 Samuel 23:14–18; Romans 8:35–39   A Friendly Reminder

THOUGHT FOR TODAY: . . . when I awake, I am still with thee. Psalm 139:18 (King James Version)

While David was hiding in the wilderness for fear that Saul would kill him, his faithful friend Jonathan came and encouraged him to put his trust in God, who was always near to help him.

I suppose that all of us have times when we are afraid. When I moved away from my home and familiar friends to a retirement home in a distant town, it was like a wilderness to me. Everything was strange and different, and I was afraid that I would never be able to adjust.

Then one day a dear friend from my church came to visit me. He did not offer any sympathy, and he certainly could not change my circumstances. Instead he strengthened my faith in God by reminding me that I had not moved away from the loving Father. We read Romans 8:35–39 together. My friend prayed for me, and I felt at peace.

PRAYER: Thank you, dear Lord, for dispelling my fear, and for reminding me that *you* are always near. Through Jesus Christ. Amen.

Mary Hamlett Goodman—San Angelo, Texas

Micah 4:1–5   When Will the "Freedom Fight" Be Over?

THOUGHT FOR TODAY: Everyone will live in peace. . . . Micah 4:4 (Today's English Version)

I remember some personal "fights for freedom" that occurred in my life before I ever heard of Martin Luther King, Jr. There was the time when I was elated to be with my mother visiting Washington, D.C. How angry I was when we detrained at Union Railroad Station and found that the "white" taxicabs could not give us a ride. The only "fight" I had then was within: the anger, the embarrassment that I dared not express!

I remember being at the march on Washington in 1963, and being thankful for the leadership of Dr. King. He helped us who had the fight for freedom in us to get it out into the open.

I look back. And I look forward. When shall the wolf lie down with the lamb and when shall we beat our swords into plowshares . . . ? (See Isaiah 11:6 and Micah 4:3, KJV.)

PRAYER: O God, I give you thanks for the life and witness of Martin Luther King, Jr. Help me to be brave in working for reconciliation and in fighting for freedom as long as necessary. For Jesus' sake. Amen.

Virginia Sargent—Ardmore, Pennsylvania   11

Matthew 6:25–34   What Is Really Important?

THOUGHT FOR TODAY: "But seek first [God's] kingdom and his righteousness. . . ." Matthew 6:33

I asked a group of people at my church to make a list of the ten most important things in their lives. When we finished I said, "Now cross off nine of them and share the one left."

One left health, saying that if you do not have health then nothing else matters. "Faith is most important to me," said another. "You couldn't live without basic faith and trust in life, the universe, and in people." "Love comes first with me," another person added. I said, "My value is the Spirit. God is Spirit! Jesus died to leave us the Spirit. The Spirit, in another person and in me, is my important value."

What is most important for you? Think about it today!

PRAYER: God, let me seek you first—your kingdom, your spirit, your love, and your justice—knowing that other things will take care of themselves. Amen.   *Richard L. Keach—Hartford, Connecticut*

Mark 15:21–30   Jesus Is in Our Lives

THOUGHT FOR TODAY: On the way they met a man named Simon ... and the soldiers forced him to carry Jesus' cross. Mark 15:21 *(Good News Bible).*

What a traumatic experience for Jesus to carry his cross from the judgment hall to Calvary!

I was in Jerusalem and set out to walk the Via Dolorosa (the way of the cross) and trace Jesus' last walk. What a spiritual experience it would be, to walk where Jesus had walked! But the spell did not last long. The path was crowded. The beggars tugged at my arm saying, 'Money?', and looked pleadingly. The noise of the crowd was disturbing to my meditation. The path was filthy with dust and trash. And some of the smells—stank! I began to resent all the intrusions.

Then I realized that it would have been exactly the same then—the beggars, all the pilgrims, the smell, the noise, the filth. Jesus is bound up with life. And he will be bound up with our lives today!

PRAYER: God, help me to be aware of you as I go about my living today. In Jesus' name. Amen.   *Richard Lawton—Adelaide, Australia*

12

Mark 5:25–34   Reaching Out

THOUGHT FOR TODAY: "Who touched my garments?" Mark 5:30

So near and yet so far" a friend wrote in a note that she tucked under my door when we were both in the same city but each going in different directions.

That phrase came back to me as I sat waiting in an airport. People were passing constantly, sitting next to me, standing beside me; but I realized how distant we were one from another, even though I could reach out and touch them. I looked across at a woman and smiled. She returned my smile, and the distance disappeared.

Because we are surrounded by people does not mean we are close to them. We need to reach out, be interested, and care.

PRAYER: Dear God, help me reach out and touch someone today and also be responsive to the touches of others. In Jesus' name. Amen.

Dathene Stanley—Chiang Mai, Thailand

1 Samuel 17:41–50   God Power

THOUGHT FOR TODAY: . . . but I come to thee in the name of the LORD of hosts. . . . 1 Samuel 17:45 (King James Version)

Goliath stomped across the valley. His huge bulk was clothed in a bronze helmet, coat, and leggings. He preceded a formidable enemy.

David, a young shepherd boy, approached Goliath.

Goliath carried a spear made of a weaver's beam tipped with a spearhead weighing approximately nineteen pounds.

David carried a sling and five smooth stones.

The outcome was evident to everyone. Except David.

"Thou comest to me with a sword, and with a spear, and with a shield: but I come to thee in the name of the LORD of hosts, the God of the armies of Israel, whom thou hast defied" (1 Samuel 17:45, KJV).

David knew what he believed.

PRAYER: Dear God, we ask you to remind us daily that no "Goliath" (problem) is too big for you. Amen.

Debra J. Walton—Lititz, Pennsylvania

13

Psalm 111:1–10   Majestic Music

THOUGHT FOR TODAY: Christ is our source of strength throughout the swirling scenes of life.

As the Communion elements were being served in our worship service, the background organ music began to convey a distinct, personal meaning to me. It was the same musical message that had consoled me during my brother's sudden funeral service in Texas. Although many years had passed, the association with this hymn was still vividly remembered. Through its lyrics and stately melody, God's reassurance had penetrated gently through my shock and sorrow.

Now this tune was still communicating God's everlasting love and utter dependability. It brought a timeless truth.

The hymn tells of "the shadow of a mighty Rock within a weary land." This Rock, our Lord Jesus Christ, is both a refuge for comfort and a base for Christian service.

PRAYER: May we abide spiritually in the shadow of Christ, the Rock, and share his comfort with the disconsolate. Amen.

Bernice Hill Borzeka—Elgin, Illinois

1 Thessalonians 5:16–22   Almost Grateful

THOUGHT FOR TODAY: The condition of being thankful brings double blessings when shared with others.

We are almost grateful." This seemed to be the way I heard the words from the radio. Of course, what the announcer had said, in a summing up at year's end, was, "We are all most grateful." What a difference I'd imparted to his words in an error in hearing!

Rushing through the days from Thanksgiving to Christmas and into the New Year may find us forgetting the attitudes of gratitude that we have just celebrated and which should undergird us from that observance through the other two. And rather than being "all most grateful," we find ourselves being "almost grateful."

I had not been careful in my listening. One hopes that that condition does not carry over into thoughtless speech. Turning the leaf to the New Year, we need to be more careful in listening, thinking, and speaking, remembering to be more than "almost grateful."

PRAYER: Lord, supplement our willingness and joy in serving with thanksgiving and praise. Amen.   *Pauline McQueen—Durant, Oklahoma*

14

Philippians 4:8–13   Living in God's Strength

THOUGHT FOR TODAY: I can do all things in him who strengthens me. Philippians 4:13

She was a frail lady, weighing less than ninety-five pounds; and she had just learned, after having gone through major surgery, that she had an inoperable cancer. Yes, she shed a few tears; yes, she had been depressed for a time. But what she lacked in size, she more than made up for in spunk, for now she was saying, "I'm not in this alone; my Lord is with me and will give me strength for whatever I have to face."

The road ahead was not an easy one for my friend, but her faith remained firm to the end. Shortly before she died, she whispered to those at her bedside, "I can do all things in him who strengthens me." And so she died as she had lived—courageously, confidently, victoriously. Her Lord had been with her all the way.

PRAYER: Lord, you alone are able to equip us to cope with our hurts and fears; may our need be your opportunity. In Jesus' name. Amen.
Rex Woods—Neenah, Wisconsin

Luke 14:25–35 The Cost of a Whistle!

THOUGHT FOR TODAY: You are the salt of the earth. Don't become diluted. Remain salty Christians! (Based on Luke 14:34)

Ben Franklin, as a boy, gave all the money in his pocket for a shiny whistle. He was proud of it until he got home and his brothers made fun of it. Suddenly, the whistle lost all its glamor and charm. He reflected on that experience when he said, "Whenever I'm tempted toward a comfortable but wrong judgment, as opposed to one that might be difficult but right, I say to myself, 'Franklin, remember the cost of a whistle!' "

As we grow in faith and commitment, we must count the cost of faithfulness. It's not enough to have an emotional glow.

PRAYER: Lord, help us to count the cost of a whistle. Help us to follow you, filled with joy, hope, and a willing life. Amen.

Arthur H. Kuehn—Lewiston, Maine

Psalm 46:7–11 Renewal

THOUGHT FOR TODAY: "Be still, and know that I am God. . . ." Psalm 46:10

I had been working several months without a day off, except the usual Saturday and Sunday. My time was filled with household duties on Saturday and church responsibilities on Sunday.

One Saturday afternoon I went for a drive in the country. As I drove through the countryside, autumn lay wrapped in her annual colorful garment.

All was peaceful—the statuesque pines, the motionless cattle, and the sleeping daisies. The tranquility of the scene permeated my soul like gentle rain falling on parched earth.

Perhaps if we would slow down and listen for God's voice to speak to our hearts, we might hear God say, "Come out into a place of solitude. Be still and know that I created you and that I alone can supply your needs and give refreshment and sustenance. Speak to me in prayer and let me speak to you through my Word. Let us enjoy sweet fellowship."

"In quietness and in trust shall be your strength" (Isaiah 30.15).

PRAYER: Slow me down, dear Lord. Help me not to be anxious or too much in a hurry; be my Pacesetter. *Ruby M. Forsberg—Lodi, California*

John 8:1–11   Risky Business

THOUGHT FOR TODAY: Or perhaps you despise his great kindness, tenderness, tolerance, and patience. Surely know that God is kind. . . . Romans 2:4 *(Good News Bible)*

None of our counselors want to work with 'religious' parents," my daughter had said. My daughter is part of a team of young women who work with pregnant teenagers in the center of the city. Although Jean is a devout Christian, she heartily agrees with her cohorts.

What is it that makes "religious" parents so difficult? I wondered. Is it because they cannot compromise or open their minds and ears to the realities about them? Have we "religious" folk set ourselves apart? Are we hanging onto the law of the Old Testament for security and forgetting the risky business of forgiveness and love revealed in Jesus Christ? Are we too quick to condemn and too slow to forgive?

PRAYER: God, strip me of unfounded self-righteousness and create within me a deepening kindness, tenderness, and patience. Amen.

Marlou MacIver—West Chester, Pennsylvania

16

1 Corinthians 12:4–11   No Coincidence

THOUGHT FOR TODAY: Bless the LORD, . . . Obeying the voice of His word! Psalm 103:20 *(New American Standard Bible)*

One morning while shaving, my husband came to me and said, "I just had the strangest feeling to pray for Butch." Butch, my cousin, is a missionary pilot in Peru. My husband prayed for him and later learned that on that same day, while flying back to his base upon completing a mission, Butch remembered a tribe whose lawnmower needed repair. He decided to check it out. Upon landing he learned of a sickness that was sweeping through the tribe. He had aboard his plane medication necessary to get the sickness under control, and many lives were saved.

It was not coincidence that Butch decided to stop there, nor was it coincidence that my husband should pray for him. God can use each of us in furthering the work of the kingdom.

PRAYER: Lord God, help my heart to be attentive and my will to be responsive to your call. For Jesus' sake. Amen.

Andrea Mondragon—Los Angeles, California

Romans 5:1–5   Anticipation

THOUGHT FOR TODAY: May the God of hope fill you with all joy and peace in believing. . . . Romans 15:13

Uncertainty and expectation are part of life. Many earthly delights are sweeter in anticipation than in actual enjoyment.

Planning a vacation or a move to a new home are times filled with excitement. Anticipation is part of the thrill of finding something new.

Sir Wilfred Grenfell said, "Where two paths are open, my principle has been to take the more adventuresome." His life bore fruits and left us the heritage of his courageous spirit and inquiring mind.

Obedience to God's call requires adventurous faith. With obedience to God's will and enthusiasm for spiritual values, we can have a glory and a glow that will outlast our years.

PRAYER: Dear Lord, help us to fulfill your purpose for our lives in the spirit of hope and anticipation. Amen.

Chloe E. Kelly—Columbia, Missouri

Matthew 25:31–40   The Face of God

THOUGHT FOR TODAY: Where is the face of God?

When you look into the faces of little children and those who need your prayers and help, what do you see?

My twin brother, who is also a minister, told me of a dream that strangely moved him. As he entered a rectangular room that resembled a museum, he was told by an angelic figure that he was going to be taken into the throne room to see the face of God. He protested that anyone who sees the face of God would be killed. He was assured that he would be safe.

The door was opened and inside stood seven people he knew: his ten-year-old daughter, his small grandson, a woman from India and her baby whom he had seen at the Church of the Nativity in Bethlehem, and his Sunday church school director with his two small children. The angelic figure turned to him and said, "My son, you have seen the face of God." He then quoted Matthew 25:40, "Inasmuch as ye have done it unto the least of these . . . you have done it unto me" (KJV).

PRAYER: Dear God, help us to see your face and your glory in the face of those who need us. Amen.   *Bennett F. Hall—Winchester, Kentucky*

John 11:28–34   Jesus Wept

THOUGHT FOR TODAY: Just "being there" is sometimes enough; for through us, God reaches out, touches, and heals heartaches.

I'm so sorry," I stammered, struggling for words to convey my sympathy to the mourning father.

Silence.

"Is there anything I can do? Anything to help?" My voice trailed off helplessly.

"You're doing it," he assured me quietly. "You're here."

Together we wept. Together we shared that deep, aching silence.

Sometimes life's burdens seem too great. The load we bear seems too heavy. But in our agony, Christ is there. He shares the sorrow, he lifts the burden, he restores our faith, he brings back hope.

Christ understands our grief, for he, too, wept.

PRAYER: Thank you, Jesus, for being with us in our times of deepest need. Amen.   *Lois E. Woods—Sumner, Washington*

2 Corinthians 12:7–10   In Weakness

THOUGHT FOR TODAY: . . . for when I am weak, then I am strong. 2 Corinthians 12:10

My hand trembled on the receiver at my first call on a telephone ministry line. Although I had been trained to listen to people in trouble, an awesome feeling gripped me. "Help me, guide me, God," I prayed.

I managed a quaky "May I help you?" A woman's sobbing voice struggled to utter her problem. I found myself saying with empathy, "Take your time; take all the time you need. I'm here to listen." I, too, needed time to empty myself of uncertainty and let God's love take over.

A half hour later, the caller's problem no longer choked her as she thanked me and said, "I feel so much better."

I felt depleted and yet strong, with a fulfilling peace and thankfulness for God's help. How wonderful to know that in weakness we find strength through our faith in prayer!

PRAYER: Thank you, God, for your bounteous love. Help me to be a channel of your love as I listen to troubled and lonely people. In Jesus' name. Amen.   *Gerda Latham—Wilmington, Delaware*

Mark 5:1–20   Included in the Symphony

THOUGHT FOR TODAY: Noticing people as Jesus did is an important goal for Christian living.

Sir Michael Costa was rehearsing with a large orchestra. Amid the thunder of the organ and the roll of drums, the player on the oboe said to himself, "In all this noise my little instrument doesn't matter," and he ceased playing. Suddenly the great conductor threw up his arms, and all was still. "Where is the oboe?" he cried.

Jesus had a knack of noticing people. There was a demon-possessed man who is unnamed in the Gospels. When encountered by this strange and frightening person, Jesus asks simply, "What is your name?" (Matthew 5:9) and brings him healing. Always he noticed people—the lonely, the frightened, the ill, the unnoticed, and the unlovely. He wanted them to become a part of the symphony of humility, each playing his or her part. Sometimes that's all others ask from us—that we notice them. Sometimes that is a lot!

PRAYER: God, help us to notice people today, particularly through the eyes of Jesus. In his name. Amen.

Charles E. Comfort—Mount Pleasant, Iowa

FEBRUARY

Ecclesiastes 3:1–11   Transitions

THOUGHT FOR TODAY: To everything, a season; for every season, an omnipotent God.

It had been a year filled with transition. Kneeling to pray one February morning, I heard the distant, yet distinctive honk of Canada geese on their annual flight north.

My heart leapt within me as I recognized this familiar harbinger of spring. The return of the geese was a fresh reminder that all was well with God's timetable of transition. The decay of winter would become spring's seedbed. Spring would find its fulfillment in the bloom of summer followed by the full harvest of autumn and the sleep of winter.

Just as the seasons ebb and flow, even so we all face seasons of transition. Locations change; loved ones move in and out of our lives. If we would know stability in the midst of flux, we must know and trust the eternal, unchanging Creator of all seasons.

PRAYER: "Change and decay in all around I see;
O Thou who changest not, abide with me" (Henry F. Lyte).

Patricia Souder—Montrose, Pennsylvania

20

Hebrews 10:19–25   Remembering the Song

THOUGHT FOR TODAY: . . . Let us consider how to stir up one another to love and good works. . . . Hebrews 10:24

There is a species of bird in Europe, so I am told, that has a beautiful song and is in much demand as a pet. However, owners have found that when one is in captivity, it soon forgets how to sing.

As Christians our "song" is to express love and do good works. The writer of Hebrews suggests that we need to assemble together to "stir up one another to love and good works."

No doubt the bird, the chaffinch, can exist in captivity long after it stops singing. But the beauty of the bird is in its song. We are here to "sing" the "songs" of kindness and helpfulness. And the church is here to help us remember the song.

PRAYER: O God of the church, help us to be faithful in our coming together to worship so that we may more effectively "sing." Amen.

Robert R. Allen—Maryville, Missouri

John 3:1–16   Religion's Missing Ingredient

THOUGHT FOR TODAY: ". . . unless a man is born of water and the Spirit, he cannot enter the kingdom of God." John 3:5 (New International Version)

I go to church on Sunday," I protested. "I try to live right. I'm as religious as you are!"

"Being religious has nothing to do with it," Bill explained. "Asking Jesus to take over your life is the only way."

Nicodemus wrestled with the same dilemma as I did. As a member of the Sanhedrin, he went through the motions of being religious, but something was missing. Then along came Jesus. He was like a breath of fresh air blowing through the musty halls of the synagogue. Nicodemus sensed the missing ingredient lay within the unusual and unorthodox person of Jesus Christ. In the quiet and privacy of a pivotal evening in the life of Nicodemus, Jesus gave him the answer to his question.

PRAYER: Lord, blow fresh air through the musty minds of those who haven't yet discovered "religion's missing ingredient." Amen.

Sandra Brooks—Clinton, South Carolina

21

Psalm 61:3   A Shelter

THOUGHT FOR TODAY: For thou hast been a strength to the poor, and a strength to the needy in his distress, a refuge from the storm. . . . Isaiah 25:4 (King James Version)

I'll race you to the covered bridge," called my sister as we hurried home from school with hail pelting our heads.

The wonderful safety and shelter of the bridge was indeed welcome. As we stood there close together in the semidarkness, my sister repeated a verse from Isaiah which she had learned in church school: "A strength to the needy . . . a shelter in the time of storm."

During the years since that day in Iowa, I have often found strength in those words of Isaiah. In times of great spiritual need, that scene comes back. I find new faith and strength in the knowledge of God's sheltering bridge of love over and around me.

PRAYER: Our God, thank you for the constantly available shelter of your protecting presence in every need or uncertainty in life. Amen.

Ione O. White—Kennewick, Washington

Matthew 18:1–4; Luke 18:15–17   As Children

THOUGHT FOR TODAY: Loving trust will please our Teacher.

As a second-grade teacher, I am amazed each school year with the trust of the children. They enter a new classroom, meet a new teacher, and are willing to spend an entire year fulfilling that teacher's wishes. Progressively, their trust turns to love. All of their energies are spent in pleasing their teacher. Jesus needs disciples who will come as children. He needs disciples with hearts filled with enough trust and love to spend their lives and energies pleasing the Teacher.

The best and most-loved teacher we have ever tried to please in this world had nothing to teach us in comparison with what Jesus has to offer. How much more of our trust, then, should be placed in him?

PRAYER: Dear God, help our trust in you to grow daily so that we may learn from you and be pleasing to you. In Christ's name. Amen.

Elizabeth Swartz—Milton, Pennsylvania

Mark 4:35–41   God's Power

THOUGHT FOR TODAY: If it had not been the LORD who was on our side . . . then the waters had overwhelmed us. . . . Psalm 124:1-4 (King James Version)

The first days at the lake had been sunny and warm. Swimmers, sailors, and water skiers enjoyed the tranquil waters. Hikers converged on the lakeside trail. But one morning we awakened to overcast skies, a steady downpour, and tempestuous winds.

Not a boat was on the lake as I walked alone. Angry waves slapped the rocky shore, splashing water in my face. The wind staggered me, but it was the most invigorating and meaningful walk I'd had all week. The elements reminded me of God's power.

We go through periods of calmness when the ripples of our lives are unruffled, and then, without warning, our world goes awry. We are struck by winds and overwhelming waves. Then it is that we appreciate the all-powerful God, the One who sustains when all else fails.

PRAYER: God, thank you for speaking peace to our troubled souls when we need you the most. In Jesus' name. Amen.

Irene B. Brand—Southside, West Virginia

Romans 3:19–26   The Accident

THOUGHT FOR TODAY: God gave the Law through Moses, but grace and truth came through Jesus Christ. John 1:17 *(Good News Bible)*

A cloud of dust rose from the median of the highway. I felt a lump in my stomach as the settling dust revealed a car on its roof, wheels spinning in the air. The lump hardened in my stomach as I approached the overturned car, and a baby's cry rang in my ears. The lump in my stomach turned to jelly as I anxiously watched father, baby, and mother safely emerge from the car.

What a difference it made in the way I drove the rest of the trip! Why is it that it takes such a tragic incident to make one act responsibly? There is nothing like witnessing an accident to make one drive safely. Laws and safety tips do not seem to be enough. We are so hard to teach, but I guess that is why Jesus Christ had to die. Laws and regulations have never been enough.

PRAYER: O God, we are sorry that we are so hard to teach. Grant us the sense to abide by the laws and safety rules of the road.

Ron Evans—Eden, Ontario, Canada

23

2 Corinthians 12:7–10   Self-Pity

THOUGHT FOR TODAY: We can all feel sorry for ourselves, but the person who accepts things as they come counts.

He loved athletics and he attended all games and practices of football, basketball, baseball, and track. Polio had laid him low. He could only walk with a cane and in sort of a rolling motion. He tired easily but learned all there was to know about the sports he loved. He always had a word of encouragement or suggestion for improvement for every player. The cheerful, keen interest in every contestant was never clouded by self-pity over his own crippled condition.

After college the young man became a high school principal and coach. When the need for a new college sports field became necessary, it was named after him. One never heard him bemoaning his handicaps, and many felt that he did more for the school's athletic program, year after year, than the most valuable player of any team.

PRAYER: Lord, let me use all the abilities I have in such a way that you can be proud of me. Amen.   *William C. Osgood—Springfield, Oregon*

Romans 8:35–39 Life's Changes

THOUGHT FOR TODAY: "As long as the earth remains, there will be springtime and harvest, cold and heat, winter and summer, day and night." Genesis 8:22 *(The Living Bible)*

I stood ankle deep in a carpet of leaves while a gloomy sky dribbled cold rain through the bare trees. The landscape seemed lifeless. Frost had blackened the ground. A frigid wind pierced my garments, and I bade goodbye to autumn, my favorite season of the year. Dejected, I plodded along the trail and soon uncovered a few overzealous spring flowers blooming under the dead leaves. Such evidence of the continuing seasons was encouraging, and I became cheerful as the raindrops turned to snow and pure white flakes dusted the ground.

Like the seasons, life isn't static, and we seem to end one experience only to start another. With Christian hope we need not dread the future, but we can look forward to each new day with expectation.

PRAYER: God, we trust you to bring orderliness to our lives, just as you guide the course of nature. Amen.

Irene B. Brand—Southside, West Virginia

Zechariah 4:1–10 Small Things Can Be Great

THOUGHT FOR TODAY: The days of small things often are the days when great things are achieved.

Most of us at some time in the routines of life have despised "the day of small things." There are household chores to do, the cows and chickens to feed, office routines to accomplish. Who of us has not wished to be done with daily puttering—to do a "big thing" just once?

Aren't the worthwhile things in life little things—a kind word, a smile, a courteous act? The Bible suggests that our smallest acts are noticed in heaven. Jesus was aware of the worthwhileness of little things. He saw the poor woman drop two pieces of copper in the contribution box. He took two fishes and five loaves from a small boy and fed the multitude. He said, "Blessed is the person who gives a cup of cold water in my name."

Small things? Trifles? They can be very great indeed.

PRAYER: God, help me not to minimize the small things in my daily routines. May I see your grace as the real thing in my life. In Jesus' name. Amen. *Raymond M. Veh—Thiensville, Wisconsin*

Ephesians 5:15–20   A Sense of Direction

THOUGHT FOR TODAY: . . . Understand what the will of the Lord is. Ephesians 5:17

A young preacher had just completed his very first Sunday service in a new community. He stood at the front door, meeting and greeting each worshiper. One of the last to leave was a very conservative, plainly dressed man with white hair and a white, well-trimmed beard. As he shook the hand of the young pastor, he said, "Young man, I like you. You know where you are going, and you know when you get there."

How important it is, not just for the preacher in his or her sermon, but for all persons to know where they are going! This sense of direction comes through soul-searching, prayer, and action taken on the basis of the best judgment God gives to us.

PRAYER: O God of wisdom, grant us a clear sense of direction so that we may walk in the way you have designed for us. In Jesus' name. Amen.

Leland Grove—Keswick, Iowa

2 Corinthians 4:7–16   We Are Never Failures

THOUGHT FOR TODAY: We are afflicted in every way, but not crushed; perplexed, but not driven to despair. 2 Corinthians 4:8

Who would consider having a holiday to honor a politician who failed in business, was defeated for the state legislature, had a nervous breakdown, was defeated for Congress twice, was defeated for the Senate twice, was ridiculed by the press, and was defeated for the vice-presidency? Yet who would not honor Abraham Lincoln, who bore all those defeats? He failed many times, but he was not a failure!

Who would hire a preacher who had severe health problems, who was considered by many to be crazy, who didn't speak eloquently, who had been chased out of town after town by angry citizens, and who had a long jail record? Yet who would not honor the apostle Paul? He failed many times, but he was not a failure.

God doesn't offer easy success. We may fail many times trying to do God's will. Yet if we are faithful, we will be more than conquerors in God's eyes.

PRAYER: God of mercy, when we get discouraged and want to give up, let us be able to turn to you for renewed strength. In Jesus' name. Amen.

Michael E. Dixon—St. Louis, Missouri

Hebrews 3:7–14   Daily Doses

THOUGHT FOR TODAY: But encourage one another daily, as long as it is called Today . . . Hebrews 3:13 (New International Version)

Prescriptions give specific directions. The one given in Hebrews is to be taken daily as long as there is a Today.

Teachers get students to work hard by saying encouraging words. When learning to walk, a child eagerly ventures toward arms extended in encouragement. Encouragement helps us to try and persevere.

It has been conjectured that if Satan had a box of "tools" and was able to keep only one, he would choose the one of discouragement.

For good "health," be generous with encouragement. Given in large daily doses it prevents many "ills."

PRAYER: Thank you, Jesus, for those people who encourage me. Remind me daily to give encouragement to others. In your name. Amen.

Peggy Berglund—Plymouth, Minnesota

26

John 3:16–17   A Bruised Reed

THOUGHT FOR TODAY: There are no throwaway people.

Wet snow was falling on downtown Philadelphia. It was early February, at noon. On Thirteenth Street there was a card shop, its cheerful window decorated for Valentine's Day. Lacy hearts and pretty verses spoke to the dismal street. Shuffling along the narrow pavement came a man dressed in ragged clothes. It was snowing on him as he stopped to look at the valentines in the window. He stayed there a long time, reading the expressions of love. Then he turned, as though coming out of a reverie, and continued on his aimless way.

First he encountered a man with a briefcase, who brushed him aside with a "get lost, you bum" gesture. The emptiness he must have felt each day is hard to imagine.

Suddenly the words of Isaiah came to me. He was speaking of the promised Messiah. "A bruised reed he will not break . . ." (Isaiah 42:3). These words echoed in my mind the rest of that afternoon. "A bruised reed he will not break. . . ." Even when I lay my head upon my pillow that night, I could still see that threadbare man.

PRAYER: Help us, dear Lord, not only to understand but to touch in love a bruised reed today, so that your healing may begin. Amen.

Carl K. Garlin—Collingswood, New Jersey

Jonah 2:1–10   Tuned In

THOUGHT FOR TODAY: Then the word of the LORD came to Jonah the second time. . . . Jonah 3:1

I called to Larry from the kitchen and asked, "Did you put out the garbage?" He replied, "Yes, I *did* put the car in the garage!" We faced each other squarely, and I repeated my question. We both laughed at the discrepancy between what I had said and what he had heard. We decided on tactics we could both use to avoid such miscommunications.

First, talk to each other directly. Second, tune out distracting background noises; third, tune in to the exact words being spoken. Such simple steps could also minimize our missed spiritual messages. To each of the seven churches Jesus said, "He who has an ear let him hear . . ." (Revelation 1–3).

PRAYER: God, open my ears so that I may hear the voice of truth you send so clear. In Jesus' name I pray. Amen.

Wonda Layton—Lynnwood, Washington

Romans 4:1–8   Comfort

THOUGHT FOR TODAY: Our sins are covered and paid for by Jesus Christ.

Last year, after a great disappointment, I turned away from God because it seemed to me that God's way and plan for my life were far from good.

Then one night, after a heavy argument, I knew I needed help and called a friend in the United States. We talked for more than half an hour, and the phone bill was very high; but it helped me in a tremendous way. At that moment the Lord used this Christian friend to comfort me. She didn't give me a long sermon or a long speech; she just told me that Peter had done the very same thing and was not much better than I was at that moment. But she also pointed out how Peter was forgiven and how he became one of the pillars on which the early church was built. That night I cried out to God, and afterwards I knew my sins were forgiven. Peace and joy filled my heart again, and I thanked God for using this friend.

Do we ever ask God to use us to comfort a friend?

PRAYER: Dear Lord, help us today to speak words of encouragement to a friend who needs it. Amen.   *John Farenhorst—Amsterdam, Holland*

Hebrews 11:32–12:2 Faith

THOUGHT FOR TODAY: . . . what is faith? Faith gives substance to our hopes, and makes us certain of realities. . . . Hebrews 11:1 *(The New English Bible)*

Ash Wednesday, the day on which Lent begins, is a good time to take stock of our faith. The writer to the Hebrews mentions people who "died in faith." Their faith is the reason we remember them. In the midst of winter we have faith that spring will come with its shrubs and flowers. As the tulips struggle through the soil, even though the earth is still cold and dry, there is hope that spring is near. Because of past experiences, we know that this is so. We believe God's promises because God has proved them so often!

Let us begin our Lenten meditations with a *fast* from negative thoughts that cause us to be weak and have a *feast* on promises that inspire! Our Bible is full of them, especially the Gospels.

PRAYER: Our God, help us to live joyfully in the hope and faith that you have given us through your Son. Amen.

Ruth H. Short—Norman, Oklahoma

28

Matthew 5:38–48 A Big Circle

THOUGHT FOR TODAY: "Love your enemies and pray for those who persecute you." Matthew 5:44

A black woman entered a train compartment and was met by hostile stares and rude comments from the other passengers. She looked into their cold eyes and thought, "Well, there's just one thing to do. I'll have to give them a smile."

It took several smiles and some kind words, but the hostility gradually changed to interest and then to friendship.

Afterwards the woman commented, "I guess you just get what you give. You give a little of yourself, and it turns out all right."

Someone else said it in another way. "He drew a circle and left me out. But love and I had the wit to win. We drew a circle and took him in." I thought about the black woman, and I hoped I would begin drawing bigger circles.

PRAYER: Dear God, help me learn to draw really big circles and fill them with lots of love. For Jesus' sake. Amen.

Dathene Stanley—Chiang Mai, Thailand

Matthew 26:3-5, 14-16; 27:3-9   Redemption

THOUGHT FOR TODAY: Evil need not triumph, for there is love. Nothing is beyond the possibility of redemption.

It isn't very pretty—an ugly plastic bag, tied with a cheap red string—but it has so much potential! Worshipers at an ecumenical Ash Wednesday service each received one, as they rose from Communion. It is a Judas bag, and it symbolizes betrayal, when one of the Twelve sold out the Master for thirty pieces of silver.

A note attached to the bag recalls that event; the note says that each receiver of the bag can redeem it and change its symbolism, if he or she chooses to do so. The Judas bag can become a "bag of love." Filled with coins, it can be given as a part of the effort to alleviate the needs of starving persons in the Third World.

Once the cross was an object of scorn; now it epitomizes love. The betrayal redeemed through acts of love? Of course!

PRAYER: God, you allowed your Son to suffer and die in order that we might be redeemed; help us to be redeemers. Amen.

Mildred Schell—Dayton, Ohio

29

Matthew 14:23-33   No Place for Fear

THOUGHT FOR TODAY: "Turn your eyes upon Jesus; Look full on His wonderful face. . . ." (Hymn by Helen Howarth Lemmel)

I can imagine Peter, excitement thrilling his body, when Jesus said to him "Come!" I can see him as he scrambled over the side of that boat and, looking straight at his Master, walked on the water toward him. But, then, he let his sights turn aside for a second and realized the ferocity of the storm and the height of the waves. Fear overtook him, and he started to sink. The chiding from Jesus concerning his lack of faith would have been bad enough, but he must have felt an awful disappointment in himself. He had let down his Lord.

What a lesson we can learn from this! When fear comes in, trust goes out. There is positively no way that trust and fear can co-inhabit our lives. But when we keep our eyes fixed on Jesus, our faith can keep us steady as we walk on troubled waters.

PRAYER: O God, may I keep my eyes on you so steadily that fear has no place in my life. In Jesus' name. Amen.

Jewell Tilden—Claremont, California

Exodus 3:7–10; 4:10–13 Someone Else

THOUGHT FOR TODAY: . . . "Oh, my Lord, send, I pray, some other person." Exodus 4:13

I'm too old. I did my share when I was younger, and now it's time some of the young mothers take the responsibility," a silver-haired lady told me when I asked her to work in vacation church school.

I asked the young mothers, but they had too many other responsibilities; so there was no vacation church school that year.

Moses was eighty when he led the children of Israel out of Egypt. He didn't think he should do it, but God did. And God was right.

Perhaps the amount of our years is not as important as the amount of our faith.

PRAYER: Dear God, when you call, help me answer. For Jesus' sake. Amen. *Dathene Stanley—Chiang Mai, Thailand*

30

2 Corinthians 4:8–18; 6:3–7 Discouraged but Not Defeated

THOUGHT FOR TODAY: "I have told you all this so that you will have peace of heart and mind. Here on earth you will have many trials and sorrows; but cheer up, for I have overcome the world." John 16:33 *(The Living Bible)*

The cause of freedom looked bleak. George Washington's troops had been defeated at Brandywine Creek and Germantown. With winter now approaching, he had no choice but to lead his demoralized and ill-equipped army into a winter encampment at Valley Forge. There things deteriorated from bad to worse—the cold, the lack of adequate shelter, the insufficiency of ragged uniforms, the absence of shoes, the unavailability of food for many.

The early Christians also faced circumstances that could have given them real reason to become discouraged and defeated. Yet the apostle Paul chose to view the difficulties he faced as opportunities to demonstrate the power of Christ. Paul chose to be an overcomer through Him who had not been defeated, even by death on a cross.

PRAYER: Lord, help us to reach to you and appropriate your power so that those things in our lives which discourage us might not defeat us. Amen. *Marlene Bagnull—Drexel Hill, Pennsylvania*

1 Corinthians 12:12–20   The One Sense We All Share

THOUGHT FOR TODAY: There would not be a body if it were all only one part! As it is, there are many parts but one body. 1 Corinthians 12:19-20 *(Good News Bible)*

Did you ever stop to consider that there is only one sense that the whole body has? It is the sense of touch.

"Touch" is the experience of the total body and, by analogy, the universal experience of the body of Christ. We all have the ability and responsibility to touch and to feel for and with one another. "Presence" is our greatest need. To be alone, even when things are going well, can be intolerable. Jesus' last words were: "I will be with you always, to the end of the age." While time lasts, while we last, Jesus will touch our lives with his presence.

PRAYER: Thank you, God, for those who touch our lives with their loving presence. And thank you, God, for never leaving me. Amen.

Frank Koshak—Prairie Village, Kansas

John 15:11–17   I Have a Friend

THOUGHT FOR TODAY: Life is broadened and deepened by our friendships.

In the face of great decisions and challenges, where do you turn for assistance? Elizabeth Barrett Browning once asked Charles Kingsley: "What is the secret of your life? Tell me, that I may make my life beautiful." "I had a friend," was his reply.

William Glasser, a practicing psychiatrist writes: "Our basic needs are fulfilled through involvement with other people. . . . At all times in our lives, we must have at least one person who cares about us and whom we care for ourselves." Many a person has been sustained in difficult hours by his or her friends.

Jesus knew the value of friendship. He said: "There is no greater love than this, that a man should lay down his life for his friends. You are my friends . . ." (John 15:13, *The New English Bible*). A personal friendship with Christ broadens and deepens all other relationships.

PRAYER: Our God, thank you for our friends. Deepen our friendships with Christ and one another. In Christ's name we pray. Amen.

Charles E. Comfort—Mount Pleasant, Iowa

John 5:2–8 Looking in All the Wrong Places

THOUGHT FOR TODAY: "Wilt thou be made whole?" John 5:6 (King James Version)

Jesus asked the lame man a simple question and got a complicated answer. The poor man had struggled with his sickness for so long that all he could talk about was his own solutions for getting healed.

Every passing year must have looked a little bleaker for him. He didn't expect that God had a plan different from his. Jesus took him by surprise, however, and healed him without lifting a finger.

Sometimes we get so mired in our problems and weighed down by our guilt that we can't hear Jesus asking us: "Do you want to be healed?" Jesus is willing to help us, guide us, heal us, and lead us.

Sometimes, what we have to do is stop all our scheming and just listen for the question, then wait for Jesus' answer.

PRAYER: Dear Lord, I know you love me. I know you hear my prayers and know of my struggles. Today I will listen for your question. Amen.

Pat Buysse—Derwood, Maryland

32

1 Kings 19:12; Psalm 46:10 Interruptions

THOUGHT FOR TODAY: We must learn to listen for the still, small voices.

From an early age I was taught never to interrupt anybody unless it was absolutely necessary. Being a shy person by nature, that was no problem. I've even gotten to the point that, unless I am in a bad mood, I automatically shut up when someone interrupts me. Usually, when that happens, I slowly get angry.

God's like that, too. God won't interrupt the everyday clutter of events in our lives unless it is absolutely necessary. God's still, small voice ceases when we rudely butt in with our own dissertations. God will forgive us but must be disturbed when we won't give God the time to speak to us.

It's up to us to interrupt ourselves and give God a chance to speak to us out of God's abundant love and wisdom.

PRAYER: Most loving God, forgive us for our uncaring and unlistening spirits. May we always give you time to speak to us. For your Son's sake. Amen.

Joe Sewell—Melbourne, Florida

Matthew 11:25–30   Show Him Your Hands

THOUGHT FOR TODAY: God gives us life, and God gives that life meaning.

In a London tenement, a young girl lay dying. Her few years had consisted only of hard labor, little love, and, finally, tuberculosis. A minister was summoned to her bedside. He told her of God's love for her, and the girl was greatly moved, for she had never before heard of Jesus Christ. She asked the minister how, when she went to heaven, Christ would recognize her. He noticed her battered, work-worn hands and replied: "Just show Him your hands. He'll know you. He'll understand."

Risk, sacrifice, and suffering are frequently the conditions of the Christian life. Yet sacrifice is converted to fullness, the risk to security, the suffering to happiness.

PRAYER: We pray that we may know ourselves as you know us, O Lord. In Christ. Amen.   *Jack Naff—Hermiston, Oregon*

Ecclesiastes 3:10–13, 5:19–20   A Spiritual Gift

THOUGHT FOR TODAY: Find enjoyment in His toil—this is a gift of God. Ecclesiastes 5:19

Although a year has elapsed, I still recall the despairing young woman's voice over the crisis line asking about training programs. "I'm mentally retarded," she said, "I want to be trained to do something. I would give anything to go to work at eight in the morning and come home at five."

Her words affected me deeply. How fortunate we are to have the desire to work and enjoy whatever we are doing. At my age of three score-and-ten, I feel overwhelmed at times with the joy of doing the simplest tasks. Twenty years ago, when I was left a widow, I prayed for engrossing work. My prayers were answered.

How true are the words in Ecclesiastes about the enjoyment of work. "For I do not count the days of my life because God keeps me occupied and I feel joy in my heart" (5:20, paraphrased).

PRAYER: Dear God, grant that all those who seek work to do may find tasks they are able to do and thus find enjoyment in life. In Jesus' name. Amen.   *Gerda Latham—Wilmington, Delaware*

MARCH

--- Day 1 ---

Romans 5:1–5; James 1:2–5   Struggles Produce Strength

THOUGHT FOR TODAY: We can rejoice . . . when we run into problems and trials for we know that they are good for us. . . . Romans 5:3 *(The Living Bible)*

We can learn a lesson from the butterfly. A young boy once observed one locked in what seemed like a hopeless struggle to get free from its now useless cocoon. Feeling sorry for it, he took a pocketknife, carefully cut away the cocoon, and set the butterfly free. To his dismay, it lay there, wiggled weakly for a short while, and died. He learned later that this was the worst thing he could have done. A butterfly needs the struggle to develop the strength to fly.

Life is full of problems. They come to everyone, and we really shouldn't be surprised when they do. In fact, we should thank God for them because going through trials can strengthen our spiritual muscles.
PRAYER: Thank you, God, that even though everything around us may be stripped away, Jesus, our strength, is still there! Amen.

Robin Lewallen—Mentor, Ohio

34

--- Day 2 ---

Leviticus 19:9–19   My Siamese Twin

THOUGHT FOR TODAY: Resentment is the opposite of praising and trusting God.

Jody pushed little Tammy down at recess, causing her to scrape her knee. That evening Tammy ranted, "I hate Jody!" With pouting lip and silence, she ate little supper and sulked all evening.

Mean thoughts tortured *me*—not the enemy I wanted to hurt. Hate isn't like throwing a rotten egg at the other fellow; it's like soaking the fabric of my own soul in garbage. Hate isn't something I hurl, it's something I become; misery fills my consciousness wherever the eye turns, on whatever the mind focuses.

This is the world of the God who is the personification of love. Love is all. I'm a spiritual Siamese twin with all people. Their welfare is my welfare. By loving them, I bless both them and myself. I must cling to my Savior to be able to love the unlovely.
PRAYER: Lord of love, become my all that I might love through a power greater than my own. Amen.   *Luther Cross—Seaton, Illinois*

Daniel 10:11–19   Love Overcomes Fear

THOUGHT FOR TODAY: . . . "God loves you, so don't let anything worry you or frighten you." Daniel 10:19 (Good News Bible)

In this passage that records Daniel's vision of the future, terror has filled his heart. Fear has left him physically weak and trembling. Even men who did not see what he saw were gripped with fear and ran and hid. Daniel, left all alone, was so overwhelmed that he literally passed out. When he came to, an angel told him *first* that God loved him. Then he was told not to be afraid.

When we know that someone truly loves us, we feel safe and secure. We can turn to that person when things get out of control and know he or she will help us. Today our future is uncertain as our world shakes in turmoil. We can worry and fear, or we can remember that God loves us. Because this is true, we do not need to be afraid.

PRAYER: Dear God, fill us with the assurance of your love and banish every fear. In Jesus' name. Amen.   *Jeri Sweany—Annapolis, Maryland*

Daniel 1:3–20   How Far Do You Go?

THOUGHT FOR TODAY: When ideals seem impractical, persons of faith continue to live by them.

Kierkegaard once likened the wayward Christians of his day to a wild duck used to the trackless wilderness of the sky. On one of the duck's migrations north he landed in a farmyard where tame ducks were being fed. He ate some of the corn and liked it so much that he lingered until the next meal. Meal followed meal, until autumn came. His old companions flew over the farm and called to him that it was time to move south. Their cry roused him to flap his wings, but he could not leave the ground to join them. Each spring and fall the cries of his former companions roused him to try to fly away, but each year the calls seemed farther and farther away. The corn was good and the barnyard secure.

Long ago Daniel faced the clash of cultures and life-styles. For him, absolute loyalty to God was the only choice. How will *we* choose?

PRAYER: Our God, when we are challenged to conform to our surroundings, give us the courage to be your people. Amen.
Charles E. Comfort—Mount Pleasant, Iowa

1 Timothy 4:1–5   When Our Backs Are Turned

THOUGHT FOR TODAY: "Go therefore and make disciples of all nations. . . ." Matthew 28:19

Not long ago I returned home from college for about a week. On Sunday I went to church there and afterwards was asked by the minister to greet the congregation at the back of the sanctuary. Near the end of the line was the mother of a boy I had taught in several youth classes and camps, and when I reached to shake her hand, she began to talk rapidly, telling me how much I had meant to her son in the past years and how grateful she was to me.

At first I was dumbfounded because I knew I hadn't had a close relationship with him. But the more I thought about it, I experienced a humbling sensation. God had used me to draw that boy closer to Christ. God had reached him while my back was turned.

PRAYER: Dear Lord, we thank you for the times you use us when we are not looking and ask guidance for the times we do turn around. Amen. *Debbie Clugy—Panhandle, Texas*

—————————— Day 6 ——————————

1 John 4:7–11   A Love That Won't Let Go

THOUGHT FOR TODAY: For I am sure that . . . [nothing] will be able to separate us from the love of God. . . . Romans 8:38–39

Over one hundred years ago, a pastor in Scotland was reviewing his memories. He did not know when the dark of evening came, for he was blind.

When as a teenager blindness came gradually to him, shadows had also come over his spirit. A girl he loved had jilted him when she realized he was going blind. He had decided never to marry. Ministry for Jesus Christ had absorbed the devotion of his brilliant mind. He had even preached for Queen Victoria.

But the old hurt was still there. Amid severe mental suffering, a four-stanza poem came to his mind: "O Love that wilt not let me go. . . ."

The great hymn words that came to George Matheson that night remind us that even when earthly lovers disappoint us, God's love will never let go.

PRAYER: Jesus, Lover of our souls, how steady is your love for us, how dependable! Thank you, Lord. Amen. *Milan Lambertson—Lakin, Kansas*

Genesis 1:26–2:3   Cocreators with God

THOUGHT FOR TODAY: Each of us is the sculptor of our own life, releasing from within us that which is created in the image of God.

It is told that the sculptor Michelangelo was one day pushing a cart containing a rough chunk of marble from the quarry to his studio. "Hey, Michelangelo," a bystander called out, "what are you working so hard for on a hot day like this?"

Michelangelo stopped pushing, and paused to mop his forehead with a cloth before answering. "My friend," he said, "while you rest in the shade, I have important business to finish. You see," he added, turning to the marble burden in the cart, "there is one of God's angels trapped in this marble, waiting for me to release him."

In a very real sense, we are cocreators with God as we take the raw materials given to us and fashion a life of loving relationships, faithfulness, and beauty.

PRAYER: Through your power and spirit, O God, release the angel trapped within me today. Amen.   *Gary L. Reif—West Lafayette, Indiana*

1 Peter 3:1–6   A Gentle, Quiet Spirit

THOUGHT FOR TODAY: . . . a gentle, quiet spirit, which is of high value in the sight of God. 1 Peter 3:4 *(New English Bible)*

Do you remember the *Reader's Digest* series, "My Most Unforgettable Character"? My husband and I had a friend who fit the caption perfectly. When I was a child, he was my pastor. I remember him as a tall, bespectacled, gentle man with a ready smile.

After I talked with him, my problems seemed to find solutions. He filled in for a missing baseball player on the fifth grade team. He changed a boy's life by providing him with a glass eye. He put his arm around a derelict with tenderness and concern.

This friend became a missionary to Africa and shared simple native foods and slept on mud floors. A man of means and social background, he quietly served God, valuing above all the prize of his high calling in Christ. People said he walked with God.

PRAYER: God, grant me a gentle and quiet spirit, that I may effectively serve you by serving others. Amen.

Helen Fricke—Greenville, South Carolina

Philippians 2:1–11   Who's Number One?

THOUGHT FOR TODAY: Do nothing from selfishness or conceit, but in humility count others better than yourselves. Philippians 2:3

He was an exceptional craftsman, artist, and scholar—a man who was better than most in any of these areas. As I was going to class, I saw him holding a door for one of the campus gardeners although his arms were full of books and the gardener's were empty. The two men, each nurtured in a culture that valued graciousness, bowed and motioned for the other to go first.

I remember the courtesy and respect each had for the other—but especially do I remember the professor who might have, on the basis of position or title, counted himself better. Without thinking any less of himself, he saw the image of God in that gardener, in each of his students, and in his co-workers. That kind of vision left no room for selfishness or conceit.

PRAYER: God, give us faith and trust so that we might trust only in you and so forget ourselves. Amen.   *Rex Woods—Neenah, Wisconsin*

——————————— Day 10 ———————————

2 Kings 6:11–17   Our Spiritual Resources

THOUGHT FOR TODAY: And my God will supply every need of yours according to his riches in glory in Christ Jesus. Philippians 4:19

Elisha's life was in danger, for he was being pursued by the king of Syria. When his servant awoke to find a hostile army surrounding the city, he became alarmed. But Elisha dispelled all fears. "Our army is bigger than theirs!" he declared. Through eyes of faith, the prophet was able to perceive that God had provided invisible support far more powerful than the horses and chariots that were arrayed against him.

We, too, have unseen spiritual resources to draw upon day by day. We have not been promised the absence of problems and difficulties which come crowding about us. But when we look to God in faith, we find that his infinite riches in Christ are abundantly sufficient to meet our every need.

PRAYER: Dear God, open our eyes that we may be more aware of the many resources of help that are available for us through Christ. Amen.
Mary Hamlett Goodman—Dallas, Texas

Psalm 19:1–6   "Praise the Lord!"

THOUGHT FOR TODAY: The sweetest of all sounds is praise. Xenophon

The heavens are telling the glory of God in every season, every moment, every day. Our three-year-old grandson, Benjamin, was taken "camping" by his dad. They pitched their tent in the backyard. After things had quieted down and many lights in the neighborhood had been turned off, they went outside to gaze at the heavens. At the sight of all the stars and the moon, Benjamin clapped his hands and yelled, "Hurrah!"

He recognized God's handiwork. A well-planned sermon could not have said it better than a three-year-old's simple, "Hurrah!"

"Praise the LORD! Praise God in his sanctuary; praise him in his mighty firmament! Praise him for his mighty deeds; praise him according to his exceeding greatness!" (Psalm 150:1–2).

PRAYER: Our God, we praise you for this wonderful world you have created for us to enjoy. May we be responsible stewards of your goodness. In Jesus' name. Amen.   *Arlena P. Hasel—Cincinnati, Ohio*

39

Hebrews 11:1–6   With Faith We Can Do It!

THOUGHT FOR TODAY: Faith, mighty faith, the promise sees and looks to God alone. Laughs at impossibilities, and cries, "It shall be done." Charles Wesley

People in the News" once featured a true story about two young men who "shoot the rapids" in a two-person canoe. One man is paralyzed—he cannot handle the oars to maneuver their craft through the choppy white waters. The other young man is strong and skilled at this tricky sport—but he is totally blind. Together they are able to achieve that which would be impossible alone.

That is like our relationship to Christ, I thought. When we put our faith in him, we, too, are able to achieve that which is impossible *alone.*

PRAYER: Lord, give me such faith in you that I, too, may do that which is not possible alone.   *Lois E. Woods—Sumner, Washington*

Luke 18:1–8   Dreams Do Come True

THOUGHT FOR TODAY: Thou has given him his heart's desire, and hast not withheld the request of his lips. Psalm 21:2

David knew about persistence. He knew the situation was hopeless unless God divinely interceded. God had given him a dream when he was a youth: he would be king of Israel. Yet when King Saul pursued him and tried to kill him, it looked as if his dream was a sham.

God has given each of us a purpose (dream) in life. We become discouraged when situations do not line up with our dreams. We make the mistake of seeing our dream mirrored in what is happening around us. The dream is still there, but we have pinned it on outward appearances.

Scripture says we ought to pray and not lose heart. Turn your faith from your own reasoning to the promise of God within you.

PRAYER: Dear God, confirm in my heart that dreams do come true when they're in keeping with your dreams for me. In Jesus' name. Amen.   *Judy Caisley—Auburn, Washington*

2 Corinthians 6:3–10   Failures

THOUGHT FOR TODAY: So let us never tire of doing good, for if we do not slacken our efforts we shall in due time reap our harvest. Galatians 6:9 *(New English Bible)*

Benji, an autistic child, went over to the table and deliberately knocked over the cup of coffee his mom was drinking. Then he knocked over a telephone table and threw a camera. Yet the next afternoon his mom and dad again took turns quietly rocking him.

I had seen Benji ten months earlier and was amazed by the progress he had made. Now he was beginning to talk, to feed himself, and to relate more to the world around him. But I suddenly wondered how many cups of coffee or similar upsets and how many hours of quiet rocking would go into his progress.

There is no other path to success than the path of learning to hurdle failure after failure. Success is there, through the power of God, but failure often comes first.

PRAYER: Dear God, help me not to be discouraged by failure or even by repeated failure. Help me to believe in success. In Jesus' name. Amen.   *Dathene Stanley—Townshend, Vermont*

Ecclesiastes 12:1–5   Days That Count

THOUGHT FOR TODAY: Remember now thy Creator. . . . Ecclesiastes 12:1 (King James Version)

How great it is that every day is different! Some persons say their days are all alike, but that just can't be. Even the weather differs from day to day, as do our moods, our thoughts, and our emotions. We do have variety in our lives, be it for good or bad.

I believe our day-to-day life is so influenced by our surroundings and our friends that we are like yo-yos. But if our lives, our hopes, our trust, and our faith are anchored in our God, we will stand firm. God is the One who is forever the same. We may sway or roll with the punches, but always our anchor holds firm in God! Praise God!

PRAYER: Dear God, help me really to be anchored in you—not just saying the words, but *really* being in you—held firm as your very own child. In Jesus' name I pray. Amen.

Wynona Shearer Willison—Waynesburg, Pennsylvania

John 21:8–17   "Do You Love Me?"

THOUGHT FOR TODAY: Let us love the Lord even more than any of the blessings he bestows.

I have often felt love toward a fish as I brought it to net, and then to our table. Love a fish? I think Peter loved the fish of Galilee. They provided him a living. They died that he might stock his home with comfortable furniture, warm blankets, food on the table, and provide for his wife and mother-in-law.

I remember a deacon of our church. One cold, drizzly morning Charles was frying fish beside Mill Creek. His son and I were breathing in the odors of burning pine and sizzling trout. I said, "Charles, I like good cooks. You are a good cook." With a twinkle in his eye, he returned, "Pastor, do you love me, or my fried trout?"

Did Jesus refer to the fish when he asked Peter, "Do you love me?" Was there a twinkle in his eye, or a tear? I'm sure he anticipated Peter's answer, "Lord, you know that I love you."

PRAYER: Please, Lord, help us to move the "fish" aside in our love for you. Amen.   *E. James Cain—Oroville, California*

Philemon 15–20   More Than a Slave

THOUGHT FOR TODAY: The Lord is my light and my salvation; whom shall I fear? Psalm 27:1 (King James Version)

On March 17 each year, many people wear the shamrock in memory of St. Patrick without knowing why. Sometimes they remember the legend that tells how he drove all the snakes out of Ireland.

History tells us that sixteen-year-old Patrick was captured by Irish pirates, taken from his English home, and set to tending the flocks of a chieftain in Ulster. Six years of slavery made him a devoted Christian. He escaped and went to France where he became a monk. In 432 a vision led him to return to Ireland as a missionary bishop. He labored there the rest of his life, about thirty years, and it is said that he found Ireland all heathen and left it all Christian. More than 300 churches were founded and 120,000 people were baptized through his efforts. Through Christ he became more than a slave—a beloved brother.

PRAYER: Lord, may we, through Christ, become more than slaves to sin. In his name we pray. Amen.   *Ruth H. Short—Norman, Oklahoma*

1 Corinthians 9:23–27   Where Are We Going?

THOUGHT FOR TODAY: Surely you know that many runners take part in a race, but only one of them wins the prize. 1 Corinthians 9:24 *(Good News Bible)*

Carolyne and I are the full office staff for a small business in a large town. Several years ago our boss suggested that we take long lunches on Fridays and enjoy different restaurants around town. We were driving toward the Salmon House (or so I thought) when Carolyne got into the left turn lane, heading in the opposite direction. I was a bit puzzled. "Where are we going?" I asked.

She looked around, then laughed. "I guess I was going home. This is where I normally turn." We steered back onto course, had a nice lunch, then headed back for the office.

But I kept thinking how easy it is, after we've set our goal on Christ, to let ourselves slip back into the old familiar ruts.

PRAYER: Lord, keep my feet on your pathway, my heart in your will, and my eyes on you. In Jesus' name. Amen.

Lois E. Woods—Sumner, Washington

Song of Solomon 1:1–6   Keeping the Vineyard

THOUGHT FOR TODAY: . . . They made me keeper of the vineyards; but, my own vineyard I have not kept! Song of Solomon 1:6

Maeterlinck recounts an old story that has much food for thought for us today. The story concerns a keeper of the lighthouse on a dangerous and isolated coast. The supply ship was long overdue, and the little community clustered about the lighthouse was in dire straits. Because he loved his neighbors, the lighthouse keeper began sharing with them his surplus stock of oil until finally the oil was exhausted, and one night the beacon on top of the lighthouse failed to burn. That very night, the belated supply ship, in attempting to make its way into the harbor, went on the rocks; and ship, crew, and supplies were lost.

In concluding the story, Maeterlinck says, "See that you give not away the oil of your lamp . . . let your gift be the flame."

If I were to offer an indictment of our age, it would be that in our activism we have allowed ourselves to be driven by external affairs and have neglected to cultivate the inner resources of personality.

PRAYER: God, forgive us for neglecting our vineyard, and help us to learn to keep well what you have given to our care. Amen.

Jack Naff—Hood River, Oregon   43

Ephesians 5:17–20   Hard Places

THOUGHT FOR TODAY: Therefore do not be foolish, but understand what the will of the Lord is. Ephesians 5:17

Serving a dying downtown church can be depressing. It is as if it is haunted by the ghost of its past greatness. Soon you begin to wonder if this is really the place where God wants you to be.

Something happened that made that situation bearable for me. High up, between the organ pipes in the front of our church, was a large picture of the head of Christ. My little girl was asked by a neighbor what her father did, and she said, "Oh, he sits next to God." I knew then that I was where I should be at that particular time. I had a Friend who was closer to me than a brother.

PRAYER: Dear Lord, when the way is rough and the going is hard and we wonder if we are really doing what you want, may we remember you never leave us or forsake us. Thank you, God. Amen.

Glenn Abbott—Sioux Falls, South Dakota

Matthew 18:12–14; 1 Peter 1:18–19 Benji's Boat

THOUGHT FOR TODAY: . . . You do not belong to yourselves but to God; he bought you for a price. 1 Corinthians 6:19-20 *(Good News Bible)*

Young Benji made a tiny sailboat and sailed it up and down the lake. One day a wind caught it, sending it far out of reach. Benji stood helplessly watching his beloved boat sail out of sight.

Weeks later he saw it in a secondhand store. He cried, "That's my boat!" But when he heard the price, his heart sank. Nevertheless, he was determined to earn the money to buy back his precious boat. With his father's help, he soon had enough. Placing the money on the counter, he clasped the boat to his chest, saying, "First I made you, then I bought you, and now you are TWICE mine!"

This is what God did for us. First, God made us. Second, God sent Jesus to buy us back. God can now say of each of God's children, "You are TWICE mine!"

PRAYER: Thank you, God, that even though we drifted away, you loved us enough to send your own Son to buy us back. Amen.

Robin Lewallen—Mentor, Ohio

Ecclesiastes 3:1–6 The Message of the Smudge

THOUGHT FOR TODAY: A time to clean and a time to leave a smudge.

On the north wall of my office are some pictures on which I meditate quite frequently. They are pictures depicting some of the couplets suggested in our Scripture reading for today. Below the pictures, to the right, there is the dirty smudge of a child's hand.

In our tidy little worlds we sometimes want to exclude those who "dirty up our walls." That dirty smudge and the handprint of a child serve to remind me that we are here as a church, not to have pretty pictures and clean walls but to serve people. The handprint shows the fingers reaching up, a call to assist persons in their stretch for faith that is a response to God.

PRAYER: Dear God, help us to use the smudges which people leave in our world as a call to love them as they are. Amen.

Robert R. Allen—Maryville, Missouri

Judges 4:1–10   If You Will Go with Me!

THOUGHT FOR TODAY: "My presence shall go with you, and I will give you rest." Exodus 33:14 *(New American Standard Bible)*

Barak was commissioned through Deborah to a difficult task. He sensed its enormity and his own weakness. He decided that he would, however, face Sisera if Deborah accompanied him.

In all of our lives there are those tasks and challenges we dread. When confronted with the problems of life, we become keenly aware of our inadequacies.

How good it is to know God understands! And as Barak was strengthened by the presence of Deborah, so we can face whatever life may hold, knowing that God is with us.

It has been said, "The will of God will never lead you where the grace of God cannot keep you." Hear God assure you: "My presence shall go with you, and I will give you rest."

PRAYER: Our God, may the assurance of your presence give us the courage to venture calmly into the difficulties of life. In Jesus' name. Amen.   *David P. Nolte—Albany, Oregon*

Luke 12:13–21   Poor in Spirit

THOUGHT FOR TODAY: "Blessed are the poor in spirit, for theirs is the kingdom of heaven." Matthew 5:3

We live in a world where selling yourself, putting your best foot forward, and getting one up on the next person is promoted in books and magazine articles. The essence of success is conveying the idea that you are more successful than you really are. Even churches want pastors who are "winners." Paul would have trouble with his image in today's world. His appearance was weak and his speech contemptible. The people who think that the world is waiting for them and their talents cannot understand what Jesus means by being poor in spirit.

Today's poor in spirit understand what was meant when the disciples asked Jesus to increase their faith. They felt so weak, so poor, so inadequate. They knew their strength came from God.

PRAYER: God, give us eyes to see differently from the way the world sees. Help us to realize our utter dependency on you. Amen.

Glenn C. Abbott—Sioux Falls, South Dakota

Romans 16:1-16   Phoebe—Friendly and Faithful

THOUGHT FOR TODAY: . . . for she herself has been a good friend to many people and also to me. Romans 16:2 (Good News Bible)

In this personal greetings section of *Romans*, Paul listed twenty-five persons by name, but Phoebe was listed first. She was a trusted friend of Paul's. To be a Christian at Cenchreae was no easy matter, for seaports during this period were extremely evil places. She was the only woman listed at that place. She was a woman with great and good influence.

Paul seems to have indicated that Phoebe devoted herself unselfishly to the ministry of the church. Indeed her industry and trustworthiness, her goodness and sympathy, her loyalty and kindness marked her as a woman whose ministry inspired all.

Just who are the Phoebes of our day? Who are the friends of Paul for Christ's sake? They are all of the sisters and brothers who live the Christlike life by their acts of friendship for others.

PRAYER: O God, help me to be a good friend to many people. For Jesus' sake. Amen.   *William W. McDermet—Indianapolis, Indiana*

Isaiah 45:1-6   That Unexpected Light

THOUGHT FOR TODAY: God sometimes uses worldly things to shine his heavenly light on us.

The pastor had just completed his hospital calls and was walking through the hall headed for the exit. The burden of those he had just seen in their pain and physical trauma tore at his mind and soul.

As he approached the exit he saw several nuns in a group talking together. When he passed by he expected to hear something pious or holy—something about faith or the church or caring for the sick. To his surprise what he heard was the question, "Who won the World Series?"

What is so amazing is that the "worldly" question so beautifully broke through the darkness of the pastor's spirit with a "holy light." The weight of human pain was lifted and God's presence was felt when those nuns reflected a fresh reality.

PRAYER: O holy Father, awaken us to your holy light shining through the common situations we encounter in life. Amen.

Robert Allen—Maryville, Missouri

Matthew 21:1–5   A Cry for Help

THOUGHT FOR TODAY: "They shall not build and another inhabit; they shall not plant and another eat. . . ." Isaiah 65:22

Hosanna! God save us!"—it was a cry wrung from the hearts of a desperate and oppressed people. That cry still rises today.

Mr. Johnson is fifty-seven. Orphaned at the age of twelve, he has worked someone else's land as a tenant farmer ever since. Payday comes once a year. Last year, after his boss man figured his annual wages, Mr. Johnson made a total of $265 in addition to the shack provided for his family. Now his health is broken. Cancer has forced the removal of his left jaw. Unable to work, he is no longer any good as a tenant. He has no land and no money to buy any. In his predicament his faith cries, "Hosanna! God save us!"

There is no immediate answer to Mr. Johnson's plight. There never will be unless concerned Christians act.

PRAYER: Lord Jesus, in your kingdom there is good news for the poor. Give me strength to work for justice this day, for your sake. Amen.

A. Roy Medley—Trenton, New Jersey

Matthew 21:12–17   How God Judges

THOUGHT FOR TODAY: He who oppresses a poor man insults his Maker. . . . Proverbs 14:31

They must have thought he would never leave. He had overthrown everything, claiming they had made the temple a den of robbers. How much money they had lost in escaped animals and lost coins! He was creating an economic catastrophe! Didn't he realize this was just business as usual? The busiest season of the year, and he had ruined it!

The cleansing of the temple is a reminder and a warning to each of us that our financial practices as individuals and nations will be judged according to the standards of God's kingdom. Precisely because of her economic sins against the poor, Judah was cast into exile. In Christ's kingdom, a people is not judged by how well the richest among them live but by how well the poorest live.

PRAYER: O God, when I consider how many live in absolute poverty, help me to repent of "business as usual." For Jesus' sake. Amen.

A. Roy Medley—Trenton, New Jersey

Mark 12:38–44   The Hidden Poor

THOUGHT FOR TODAY: ". . . you shall not harden your heart or shut your hand against your poor brother. . . ." Deuteronomy 15:7

You had to look hard to see her. Dressed in wash-faded hand-me-downs, she would hang back, her head bowed in perpetual apology. She was the poorest girl in school. We hardly noticed her.

That day in the temple, how many people noticed the widow? Poor and unimportant, she slipped in and out unnoticed, except by Jesus.

We seldom see the poor. Hidden away in ghettos, migrant camps, and Third World countries, they are the silent cogs which turn the great wheels of our society. They pick our vegetables, mine our copper, and fill our minimum wage jobs. Their poverty guarantees that I get the cheapest prices possible. Have I chosen to blind myself to their suffering that I might live well?

PRAYER: O God, open my eyes that I might see those in misery around me and, seeing them, respond to their plight. In Jesus' name. Amen.

A. Roy Medley—Trenton, New Jersey

48

Matthew 25:31–40   How We Serve

THOUGHT FOR TODAY: So faith by itself, if it has not works, is dead. James 2:17

Here is one of Jesus' clearest charges about our responsibility toward the poor. How we carry out that responsibility is of the utmost importance.

As we approach the problem of poverty, we should not see Jesus as present in the poor primarily as an object of our generosity.

Our culture has taught us to view the poor as failures. Christ teaches us to view them as himself. Therefore, we do not come as the rich, but as the poor, to learn of God. Only as we see with the eyes of the poor, hear with the ears of the poor, and share their lives as equals will our actions be redemptive. In committing ourselves to service with the poor, let our first response to Christ in them not be "Here, Lord, a cup of cold water for you" but "Speak, Lord, for thy servant heareth."

PRAYER: Jesus, you have chosen what is weak to shame what is strong. Make me attentive to your voice in the poor, for your sake. Amen.   *A. Roy Medley—Trenton, New Jersey*

Matthew 26:20–29   Communion and the Hungry

THOUGHT FOR TODAY: "Is not this the fast that I choose . . . to share your bread with the hungry . . . ?" Isaiah 58:6-7

Incarnation makes religion a messy affair. It means that Christian faith can never be purely spiritual. It is of necessity linked with a stable and with the cross—with life.

Breaking bread and sharing the cup are likewise never separate from the material needs of others, especially the hungry. The Lord's table is a world table. With us are sisters and brothers from Haiti, India, Mali, and elsewhere. Ten million of them will die from hunger this year. They represent a majority of the world; we represent only 6 percent. Yet, we consume 35–40 percent of the world's nonrenewable resources—resources which could be used to meet their basic needs if we did not demand so much. There is great truth to the fact that we need to live simply that others might simply live!

PRAYER: O Bread of Life, help me ever to choose life for others over wealth for myself, in the name of Christ. Amen.

A. Roy Medley—Trenton, New Jersey

APRIL

Matthew 26:6–13   Troubling Words

THOUGHT FOR TODAY: ". . . You shall love your neighbor as your-self." Matthew 22:39

You always have the poor with you." Such troubling words! What are we to make of them? Do they mean that our efforts to end the suffering of the poor are doomed to failure?

In establishing Israel as a just and righteous people, God made provision through humanitarian codes and the Year of Jubilee that none might be forever impoverished. To them God promises, ". . . there will be no poor among you . . . if only you will obey the voice of the LORD your God . . ." (Deuteronomy 15:4–5).

No, rather than prophecy, Jesus' words become a judgment against any society of people where there is a perpetual underclass of the poor. The existence of entrenched poverty in any country is a sign of failure to manifest the love of God revealed in the cross of Jesus.

PRAYER: Lord Jesus, teach me to live in the truth that your death is as much for the poorest as for the greatest. In your name I pray. Amen.

A. Roy Medley—Trenton, New Jersey   51

Matthew 27:57–61   Use of Wealth

THOUGHT FOR TODAY: ". . . a man's life does not consist in the abundance of his possessions." Luke 12:15

While we scorn poverty, it was riches which Jesus constantly warned us against. ". . . How hard it is for those who have riches to enter the kingdom of God!" (Luke 18:24).

From Joseph of Arimathea we can learn how God wishes us to use wealth. First is to recognize that even that which we have set aside for ourselves belongs to God. We are never owners but always stewards, and we will be held accountable for how we carry out that charge. Secondly, whatever is used for Christ is used wisely. The highest use of our money is in behalf of others. As Christians we believe our lives are measured not by what we have but by what we give.

PRAYER: Lord, grant that whatever I have received from you I might use wisely as a faithful servant of Jesus Christ. In his name. Amen.

A. Roy Medley—Trenton, New Jersey

Matthew 28:1–10   The Easter People

THOUGHT FOR TODAY: "But seek first his kingdom and his righteousness, and all these things shall be yours as well." Matthew 6:33

The early church amazed the world with its new way of life. Most astounding was the offering for the relief of the Jerusalem church. In collecting the offering, Paul explained the new order among the Easter people: ". . . since you have plenty at this time, it is only fair that you should help those who are in need. Then, when you are in need and they have plenty, they will help you. In this way both are treated equally" (2 Corinthians 8:14, *Good News Bible*).

We are the Easter people. Through the resurrection of Jesus we have passed from death to life. Freedom to share my wealth is a sign of that life, for I know my destiny is in God's hands. What a needed witness in a world which worships wealth as the supreme deity!

PRAYER: Risen Lord Jesus, when I trust more in wealth than you, remind me of the primacy of your kingdom. In your name I pray. Amen.

A. Roy Medley—Trenton, New Jersey

Psalm 23   Still Waters

THOUGHT FOR TODAY: He leads me beside still waters; he restores my soul. Psalm 23:2–3

The previous workweek had been demanding, and I was exhausted. When Sunday afternoon rolled around, all I could think of was taking a nap. However, my daughter had other plans. She begged for a long walk to her favorite spot, a small creek not far from home.

Rachel gathered little rocks along the way to throw into the sluggish current. Every time she bent to discover another rock, I felt nothing but impatience. While I waited and she threw her pebbles, I began looking at the many still places in the stream. How tranquil! Time peacefully slipped past until, almost regrettably, it was time to leave.

Reminded of Psalm 23, I thought of those still waters and believed once more that God was directing my life, leading me through my daughter to that quiet creek to calm me down.

PRAYER: Dear God, help us to take time to be with those around us in finding the calm waters of our lives. Amen.

Jane Hursh—Ft. Myers, Florida

Matthew 6:23–24   Respite

THOUGHT FOR TODAY: "Be still, and know that I am God." Psalm 46:10

The bus sped along on the return trip from the shopping mall to the city. Quite unexpectedly, it became caught in a traffic snarl.

With a sigh, I looked through the window at a heavily wooded area. I had seen that area often, but never before had I noticed the cheerful stream bubbling along at the foot of the rocky incline. I smiled to myself as I began to enjoy this sudden visit to the "country" and to my childhood. Beside the stream were blackeyed susans, a favorite flower I often had picked as a gift for my mother.

I had gone shopping to escape the doldrums. Now I remembered other times and places and folk I cherished. Tensions ebbed. The bus began to move. Refreshed, I turned from the window and began to plan for tasks which now seemed quite manageable.

PRAYER: Keep us aware of our roots, dear God, and help us to be roots for others. Amen.   *Mildred Schell—Dayton, Ohio*

Hebrews 10:1–17   Forgiven, It Is Forgotten

THOUGHT FOR TODAY: You must forgive . . . just as the Lord has forgiven you. Colossians 3:13 *(Good News Bible)*

A woman known for her truthfulness claimed to have seen the Lord on numerous occasions. Because of her reputation, her claims were brought to the attention of the bishop. He hit upon a way to test the validity of her report.

When she appeared before him, the bishop asked, "When you see the Lord, does he talk to you?" "Yes," she replied. "All right," said the bishop. "When next you see the Lord, ask him what the bishop's great sin was before he became a bishop."

Months later the woman returned. "Have you seen the Lord?" asked the bishop. She nodded. "Well, when you asked him about the bishop's great sin, what did he say?" The woman smiled, her face filled with wonder. "He said, 'I don't remember.' "

PRAYER: Dear God, our forgiving Lord, teach us the lesson of forgetfulness, the other half of forgiveness. In Jesus' name. Amen.

Mildred Schell—Dayton, Ohio

Acts 2:1–4   The Power House

THOUGHT FOR TODAY: I am sure that neither death, nor life, nor angels. . . . nor anything else in all creation, will be able to separate us from the love of God in Christ Jesus our Lord. Romans 8:38–39

Both Old and New Testament writers mention the wind many times, usually as a destructive force. But the wind can also be used constructively. Paul uses it as a symbol of God's power.

For many years I lived in a plains area where the wind blew constantly. It turned the wheels of the windmills which brought clear, cold water from great depths; it provided power for small generators which supplied homes with electricity; and it kept the temperature at a bearable level in the hot summers.

We cannot control the wind; it blows where it will. But we can harness it for good use. Just so, many of life's inevitables are beyond our control, but often we can use them for good if we let God's power work through us.

PRAYER: God, use us to think constructively as we apply the forces of your world to our daily living. In Jesus' name. Amen.

Ruth H. Short—Norman, Oklahoma

Psalm 27:1–8   "God's Up All Night"

THOUGHT FOR TODAY: "Do not fear, only believe." Mark 5:36

In William Faulkner's book *The Reivers,* Boss was preparing to leave for a funeral. He spoke to the boy who was to stay home: "I know you are sometimes afraid to sleep in your room by yourself. Don't be. Trust in the Lord. He's up all night."

One night I found myself alone in a large, poorly locked frame house. The wind whipped around the corners, seeming to take keen delight in shaking parts of the house near my bedroom. Frankly, I found it hard to go to sleep, even though I had trusted myself into God's care.

Many people today are living lives of terror because of crime on our streets. All of us could find comfort in the reading given by a small tyke, Barney, at a church banquet, in which several lines repeated the words "Be not afraid. God's up all night!"

PRAYER: Dear Lord, help me to trust in you to the extent that there is no need to fear. In Jesus' name. Amen.

Arlena Hasel—Cincinnati, Ohio

Psalm 23   Blessings

THOUGHT FOR TODAY: Surely goodness and mercy shall follow me all the days of my life. . . . Psalm 23:6

Reread the above Scripture and let the magnitude of this blessing jar your mind. Let it pulse in your thoughts over and over again.

Take these familiar words with you today and carry them uppermost in your mind. Repeat them in the stress of your work at the office, in the tensions of a classroom, or in the clutter of a kitchen. Let this reassuring blessing calm your spirit.

Besides the benefits of goodness, we are to receive mercy. What joy! Even though we may make errors in judgment, embarrassing blunders, impatient remarks, or we may burn the biscuits, we are to be treated with compassion and forgiveness. May the thought of this healing comfort also sustain us.

PRAYER: Our God, we thank you for the blessings which help us to walk with confidence through each new day. Amen.

Mary A. Magers—Portland, Oregon

Psalm 37:1–9   Worry

THOUGHT FOR TODAY: Give yourself to the LORD; trust in him, and he will help you. Psalm 37:5 *(Good News Bible)*

Worry does not change the past nor help the future. It only takes away the strength we have to meet today's problems.

A friend who was an expert worrier said, "I gave up my worries when I realized that 50 percent of them were concerned with past events which I could not change, and 45 percent were concerns about the future events which might not even happen. The remaining 5 percent I decided to turn over to the Lord, who knows how to deal with them better than I can."

My friend discovered the reality of the truth which the psalmist shares with us in our "Thought for Today." Like her, many of us have experienced the help and power of the Lord as we gave ourselves to him in faith and trust. I wish for you the life-changing experience of such a discovery.

PRAYER: O God, I put my hand in yours in faith and trust, knowing there is nothing that we cannot handle together. Thank you. In Jesus' name, amen.

Jack E. Jones—Milwaukee, Wisconsin

Psalm 25:4–10   Being Teachable

THOUGHT FOR TODAY: ". . . he may teach us his ways and . . . we may walk in his paths." Isaiah 2:3

As the six-year-olds enter their Sunday church school room each week their eyes sparkle. Almost in chorus their excitement fills the air telling "Dad has a new job," or "My sister has a goofy new boyfriend," or "Look, teacher, I scraped my knee." Such personal opportunities to *teach* the ways of God enable children to *walk in his paths.*

Why? Because boys and girls come to God's house expecting something to happen. They love it when their teacher listens to each story and responds in an understanding manner. Sometimes it's with words: "Yes, I know that cut really hurt." Sometimes it's with a gentle hug, and sometimes with smiling eyes. What a thrill it is to be a teacher and influence others for Christ.

PRAYER: Dear God, may my walk with you be reflected in all I teach. In the master Teacher's name. Amen.   *David E. Cloud—Wichita, Kansas*

Psalm 121   God's Strength

THOUGHT FOR TODAY: I will lift up my eyes to the hills. From whence does my help come? Psalm 121:1

I have always loved Psalm 121, even when I was a little child. I used to look at the hills and mountains as we took trips in New York State.

When we moved to California, we were surrounded by hills and mountains. My husband and I used to sit at dusk and watch the deepening shadows creep over the hills and the twinkling lights come on in the homes. We would breathe in deeply the beauty of the night and the stars and be content.

Now the hills have a very special meaning to me. My beloved husband passed away. Now I stand alone at my back door and look to the mountains and pray for the strength to carry on as he would have me do. When I drive the freeways at night, I look at the lights on the mountains and have a feeling of security and peace. I know that my beloved is with God who gives help, comfort, and strength.

PRAYER: Thank you, God, for the strength to carry on. Help me to do those things that give joy to others. For Jesus' sake. Amen.

Aletta J. Streeter—Irvine, California

Matthew 1:20–23   What's in a Name?

THOUGHT FOR TODAY: . . . his name shall be called Wonderful, Counseller, The mighty God, The everlasting Father. . . . Isaiah 9:6 (King James Version)

What's in a name? Names tie a family together. Surnames give clues on ethnic background and occasionally on the original family location or occupation. First names may tell of family relationships or friendships or even the events or hopes of the parents at the time of the child's birth. Unusual nicknames nearly always have a special tale.

The name God chose for his only begotten Son reveals much. The name Jesus means "Jehovah saves." In Jesus' name and life God pours out his love, his purpose, and his character. "Christ" is a title of authority, both conferred and earned by Jesus.

How glorious, yet how humbling, to realize that believers live "in his name" and that he grants to us the title of "saint" and the family name "Christian"!

PRAYER: Lord Jesus, please bring honor to your name through me. For your sake, I pray. Amen.   *Bonnie P. Yake—Fort Wayne, Indiana*

2 Corinthians 4:8–18   Seeing Beyond

THOUGHT FOR TODAY: So we do not look at what we can see right now, the troubles all around us, but we look forward to the joys in heaven which we have not yet seen. 2 Corinthians 4:18 *(The Living Bible)*

It was the first day of spring. I wrapped my coat more tightly around me as I walked briskly to the car.

"It's anything but springtime," I grumbled.

The sky was a wintry gray, and the wind was biting. I brushed flakes of snow off the windshield.

Then I heard birds chirping. Their song penetrated the coldness of the day and the chill in heart.

Spring was here! That was a fact that even a blizzard could not change. The birds knew it. They had returned and were singing a joyous chorus despite the chilly wind.

PRAYER: Lord, teach me the secret of looking beyond present circumstances. Fill me with anticipation that the best is yet to be. Amen.

Marlene Bagnull—Drexel Hill, Pennsylvania

Job 19:21–27   The Power of Words

THOUGHT FOR TODAY: ". . . for by your words you will be justified, and by your words you will be condemned." Matthew 12:37

Evidently Job felt his words worthy of immortality. And so they were! Although not written in rock, his words found a still more enduring medium—the Word of God, which shall stand forever. I doubt that Job realized the influence his words would have on future generations.

Do we realize the power of words we uttered yesterday and of those we will speak today? Words once spoken can never be taken back, and they have great power to uplift and praise or degrade and wound the heart. Oh, that today our lips would be controlled by the Holy Spirit, that lives we touch would be blessed! The wounds we've caused are so deep—Lord, heal them! The potential for good is exciting—Lord, use us! Yet we must remember that it is yielded lips he will control.

PRAYER: Lord, speak through me that my words may be worthy of you, for they will be written in the hearts of others. Amen.

Georgia E. Hamlin—Taunton, Massachusetts

Romans 12:9–16   Nurture—A Full-time Job

THOUGHT FOR TODAY: Anxiety in a man's heart weighs him down, but a good word makes him glad. Proverbs 12:25

A pastor was heard to remark that there aren't many places a minister and his family can turn when they are troubled. All people experience hurt, weakness, and despair.

The Lord is ever-present, but even he depends on his followers to be his instruments in giving sustenance. Ministry is not confined to those who pass through the ordination council, wear a turned collar, or preach a sermon. The sensitive Christian responds in love and support even to those he or she perceives as strong. For love as taught by Jesus is a two-way path: giving in strength, receiving in vulnerability. Nurturing our neighbors as God directs is a full-time occupation for those of us who claim Christ's love.

PRAYER: Eternal God, may we profess abiding faith through our response to troubled hearts and weakened lives. In your love, amen.

Laura Lee Marques—Factoryville, Pennsylvania

Galatians 5:22–25   Power for Living

THOUGHT FOR TODAY: "How blest are those who know their need of God; the kingdom of Heaven is theirs." Matthew 5:3 *(The New English Bible)*

A friend called on the phone. She was going to town and wondered if she could get me something. I thought about what I needed. "If you find some energy," I said, "get me some, or bring me some patience or wisdom or love."

I hung up the phone and smiled. Some needs are found in stores, but other needs cannot be found in any store. I knew what I needed. My needs could only come out of a quiet time with God. I had tried to force patience and love into my days, but it hadn't worked. But when I took time to let God fill me richly with God's Spirit, then the patience and love were automatic.

I realized that I had to find more time in my life for that quiet time. I needed more "power for living."

PRAYER: Dear God, fill me today with your Spirit, for I know it is you I need to fill me with the power I lack. In Jesus' name. Amen.

Dathene Stanley—Townshend, Vermont

Matthew 28:16–20   Where's God?

THOUGHT FOR TODAY: ". . . lo, I am with you always, to the close of the age." Matthew 28:20

As my little three-year-old grandson, Aaron, was placing the little animals in his toy "Noah's Ark," he kept looking around as if searching for another character and finally asked, "Where's God?" He knew that God belonged in the ark, too.

Aaron's father explained to him that there was not a character to represent God. He asked Aaron if he remembered the day they were outside and the wind was blowing very hard into their faces. He then explained to Aaron, "We could not see the wind, but we knew it was there. That is the way it is with God; we don't see God, but we know God is always there."

PRAYER: God, help us to remember that we are never alone. You are always beside us. Amen.   *Josephine Garner—Ravenna, Texas*

Genesis 1:26–31 Let God's Image Through

THOUGHT FOR TODAY: Let God's image show through you.

A traveler one day stopped to watch a wood-carver at his bench. He noticed that the carver had no patterns for his work. Neither had an outline of the figure to be carved been made on the wood block.

"Don't you use a pattern?" asked the traveler.

"No," replied the artist. "You see, the figure is already in the block. I just chip away the wood around it."

We are quite like the carver's blocks of wood. We have God's image upon us, but too often it is marred by bad habits and faults so that it does not show through. As the wood-carver does, we must chip away those mars—bickerings, faultfinding, bad temper, etc.—so that the image of God can come through.

PRAYER: Thank you, God, for making us with the possibility of becoming like you. Help us to radiate your love to others. Amen.

Mabel A. McCaw—Des Moines, Iowa

Mark 10:13–16 Finding, Finding, Finding

THOUGHT FOR TODAY: Children add activity to faith.

The children, about thirty five-year-olds, were in the kindergarten in the city of Kweilin in China. They were well-dressed, and when we arrived, they were singing and performing a group dance.

At a certain time, one or more of the children withdrew from the group but kept on singing as they approached us, the spectators.

The children were singing in English, "Finding, finding, finding—I have found a friend; now let's go dancing." And so we did with some of them.

The theme of friendliness was repeated many times with me and others on the streets of China cities, and a warm hello has replaced the hostility and enmity of other days.

Cordiality between people of different nations can often begin with the warm friendship of little children.

PRAYER: Lord, help us to appreciate the possibilities in children and their help in making a friendlier world. In Jesus' name. Amen.

V. Carney Hargroves—Philadelphia, Pennsylvania

Matthew 6:1–15   Calm Assurance

THOUGHT FOR TODAY: "Let not your hearts be troubled; believe in God. . . ." John 14:1

Brothers Jeff and Kurt, happily playing with their model train, were visibly annoyed by sister Amy's intrusion.

"But can't I play too?" pleaded the three-year-old.

"Not now. Go on, play with your new dolly," Jeff mumbled.

With tears welling up, Amy continued to watch. Finally the force of Jeff's words struck. She stood up, smoothed her dress, walked purposefully to her chair, and quickly turned it to face the wall. Then she picked up her imaginary phone and "dialed" her friend.

No fuss, no pronouncements; Amy handled the situation well. Though childlike, the scene spoke volumes. Has not Jesus taught us similarly? We should straighten out our confused thoughts, enter our secret room, and talk to God in quiet confidence.

PRAYER: God, help me calmly to talk out my problem with you before temptation bids me to act wrongly. In Jesus' name. Amen.

Louise Sperb—Oakland, California

Ecclesiastes 11:1–6   Light a Fire: Leave It Burning

THOUGHT FOR TODAY: . . . nothing you do in the Lord's service is ever useless. 1 Corinthians 15:58 *(Good News Bible)*

How exciting to watch as the Olympic flame is ignited and then to see it extinguished as the games ended!

Several hundred persons gathered in Earlham Hall for a banquet. Across the fireplace glowed a message in gold: "They gathered sticks and lighted a fire and left it burning." Elton Trueblood recounted the story: A group of Quakers bound for the New World were delayed by mechanical problems with their ship. Repairs would take several days. Instead of complaining, these Friends went ashore and shared their faith with those who lived in that part of England. When the the ship was seaworthy again, they reboarded and continued on their journey. As such "fires" are kindled and left burning, the flame of faith spreads.

PRAYER: Lord, as we have received the flames of Pentecost, through faith fires kindled by others help us to light fires and leave them burning. For Jesus' sake. Amen.   *Mildred Schell—Dayton, Ohio*

————————————————— Day 23 —————————————————

Psalm 119:97–104   Food That Satisfies

THOUGHT FOR TODAY: How sweet are thy words to my taste. . . . Psalm 119:103

Arthur, the eight-foot boa, finished eating the live rat and coiled up contentedly. Sammy, the Siamese cat, lapped up the last of the milk and searched out a spot of sunlight to take his after-lunch nap. Barney, the dog, wolfed down his favorite meal of meat scraps and sweet potatoes. All our pets ate and were content, not eating just anything, but their own food.

For our "spiritual" food, we humans devour light reading, world news, TV, and trivial conversation and wonder why we feel something lacking in our lives. Even good educational reading, important in its place, will not satisfy deep spiritual hunger. Only a substantial amount of God's Word will give deep contentment and a balanced mental diet.

PRAYER: Help us, Lord, to guard our minds, taking in only the spiritual food that gives healthy growth and your contentment. In Jesus' name. Amen.   *Millie Lyon—Yarinacocha, Peru*

62 ————————————————— Day 24 —————————————————

Luke 8:5–15   Vandalism

THOUGHT FOR TODAY: And let us not grow weary in well-doing, for in due season we shall reap, if we do not lose heart. Galatians 6:9

Some months ago while watching television I was surprised and heartened to see former President Carter wearing a hard hat and working in a vandalized apartment house in New York City. He and other volunteers were trying to restore the building so that it could again be used for low-income families. It looked like an impossible task, but Mr. Carter was smiling, saying that it was much improved.

Vandalism has become one of the plagues of our society, and it is so easy to throw up our hands and ask, "What's the use?" Yet here was a former president believing that one person could make a difference.

So often the difficulties we face seem insurmountable, and because we're afraid of failure, we do nothing. Let us take heart in Paul's admonition to the Galatians. One person *can* make a difference.

PRAYER: Dear God, help us to believe that our efforts to improve our homes, our communities, and our world are not in vain and that one person's work can make a difference. Amen.

Bessie Bortner Scherer—Glen Rock, Pennsylvania

Jeremiah 15:15–18   Jeremiah's Pride

THOUGHT FOR TODAY: Are we serving God or ourselves?

Jeremiah began living a lifestyle for God's glory. Before long he was living this lifestyle for his own glory. Jeremiah made a career out of pain and suffering. By doing so, he began to feel sorry for himself and felt that he had given up much which God didn't appreciate.

We need to ask ourselves, "Why do we do the things we do?" For God's glory? Do we consider what God wants? Or are they done for our own satisfaction, so we can feel good about ourselves?

What had God asked Jeremiah to do in the first place? God had simply told Jeremiah to "Go and proclaim in the hearing of Jerusalem, Thus says the LORD . . ." (2:2). Jeremiah had made his faith a tiresome duty; thus he was very bitter. Are we serving the things of religion rather than the God of our faith?

PRAYER: Dear God, help us to keep you at the center in our lives so that our faith may not become burdensome. Amen.

Glenn A. Hamer—W. Baden Springs, Indiana

63

Matthew 6:28–34   Flowers: God's Smiles

THOUGHT FOR TODAY: Lovely flowers are the smiles of God's goodness. Wilberforce

As I walked in our marine garden one morning, I was charmed by a row of azalea bushes all in bloom, flanked by a double row of irises. In their midst a hawthorn tree was in full bloom. There flashed into my mind another morning of several years ago when I stood among "the lilies of the field," overlooking the Sea of Galilee. Instinctively, at that time, I had told myself, "This is the scene that Jesus saw as he assured his gathered disciples of God's care for them."

This particular morning, Easter having just passed, among the flowers in our marine garden I felt the living, loving presence of the risen Jesus assuring me of God's continuing love and care for all his children.

John Calvin Slemp has well said, ". . . and from the sod leap up ten thousand arguments for God."

PRAYER: Dear God, as we look at earth's lovely flowers, alert us to the smiles of thy everlasting goodness. Amen.

Herbert E. Hinton—Red Bank, New Jersey

Genesis 1:26–31   A Little Child Shall Lead Them

THOUGHT FOR TODAY: Jesus said, Suffer little children, and forbid them not, to come unto me: for of such is the kingdom of heaven. Matthew 19:14 (King James Version)

My grandson Landon Carter, who is four years old, lives only a short distance from my home. Quite often he visits and when he is playing, and for no apparent reason, he stops, puts his arms around me, and says, "Granddad, I love you."

Several weeks ago my wife and I were on vacation at the beach with Landon. It was interesting to notice the waves as they rolled in, and they seemed to be getting closer to Landon. Finally the waves completely surrounded him and the sand houses he was building. As he turned and looked at me, I noticed that his little face beamed with joy and happiness as he said, "You know, it feels good every time."

PRAYER: Our God, today, perhaps more than ever before, we need the perfect faith of a little child. Strengthen this faith in us that we may know Christ better, and manifest him to the world in which we live. In Jesus' name. Amen.   *Garnett R. Poindexter, Jr.—Richmond, Virginia*

James 5:13–18   Music in God's Ears

THOUGHT FOR TODAY: Is any one among you suffering? Let him pray. Is any cheerful? Let him sing praise. James 5:13

Have you ever been asked about the inefficiency of prayer? I have been. My questioner asked, "Since God knows what we have need of before we ask and so many people are all praying for the same things, isn't that awfully inefficient?"

Then I thought of prayer from God's viewpoint. He loves the sound of his children's voices. It is like music to him.

Music can be very inefficient. Think of a symphony for instance. For long passages the oboe players do nothing. The violins all play the same note at the same time.

Prayer may appear to be wasteful and at times foolish, but God loves it and he shows his pleasure by answering. Are you providing God with music regularly?

PRAYER: Thank you, God, for hearing our prayers and desiring our communication with you. Amen.   *Roger E. Compton—Springfield, Illinois*

1 Samuel 14:1–14   Expect Great Things

THOUGHT FOR TODAY: ". . . it may be that the LORD will work for us. . . ." 1 Samuel 14:6

Jonathan was a man of faith. He knew God and knew what God could do. His statement ". . . there is no restraint to the LORD to save by many or by few" (1 Samuel 14:6, KJV) reveals his faith in the Lord's power.

He was not brash as many label him. He had a plan, and he worked it. His plan was simply to ask the Lord's direction in relation to the enemy and then to obey it. He trusted in the Lord's direction.

It was not something for show, for no one knew of it. He was a man of faith, expecting God to do something in the situation.

Are you expecting God to work in your life today?

PRAYER: Dear God, help me today in faith to expect your hand to work in my life, my situation. In Jesus' name. Amen.

Garry L. Close—Plainfield, Indiana

Exodus 3:7–12   "Who, Me?"

THOUGHT FOR TODAY: But Moses said to God, "Who am I that I should go to Pharaoh, and bring the sons of Israel out of Egypt?" Exodus 3:11

Ordinary people in ordinary churches are changed into extraordinary persons when they respond to God's call. After responding, however, we often begin to have doubts about our abilities as we begin our new tasks. Though a connection has been made, no change occurs and no word comes, somewhat like a telephone conversation when one party cannot be heard.

Yet God's promise to Moses comes to each of us, for the One who promised to be with Moses is with us also. He always answers our "Who, *me*?" with a powerful "Yes, *you*!" and the promise "I will be with you." Even doubting Moses and persons like us can be used by God.

PRAYER: O God, remind us even in the midst of our doubt that you are with us. Amen.   *Eric C. Holmstrom—Issaquah, Washington*

MAY

Isaiah 58:6–9   Where Would You Be?

THOUGHT FOR TODAY: "Why do you look at the speck of sawdust in your brother's eye and pay no attention to the plank in your own eye?" Matthew 7:3 (New International Version)

There is going to be a township meeting tonight concerning a nearby church's plan to become a temporary shelter for the homeless and a counseling service for alcoholics, drug addicts, and runaways.

Our people are coming together to protest this program. They believe it is a worthy project, but they do not want it here. Consider the riff-raff that will be passing through those doors! Consider the potential danger to ourselves and our children!

If it's money to Africa or an orphanage in New York City, we are a compassionate people. But if it directly affects us, what then?

Where would you be if such a question came up? Protesting at the township meeting or volunteering down at the church?

PRAYER: Lord, stretch us so that we may serve others with joy, knowing that we must be a servant people to follow our Lord. Amen.

     Marlou MacIver—West Chester, Pennsylvania

Philippians 1:19–26   This World Is Not My Home

THOUGHT FOR TODAY: I am hard pressed between the two. Philippians 1:23

As a youngster, I often sang the chorus "This world is not my home, I'm just a passin' through. . . ." It was easy to sing about heavenly joys, for I was young and still had many years ahead of me. But as a young adult I had a serious illness that could have led to an early death. I could no longer sing, "This world is not my home," for it *is* my home, and I care very much about living out my life in *this* world.

That's part of the human situation for Christians: we are "in the world, but not of it." We often get caught in our conflicting feelings about them.

PRAYER: Lord, sometimes we don't know how to live when we are torn between our desires and our hopes; show us the way. Amen.

Rex Woods—Neenah, Wisconsin

Ephesians 2:11–18   Walls and Peace

THOUGHT FOR TODAY: For he . . . has broken down the dividing wall of hostility . . . so making peace. Ephesians 2:14-15

In his poem "Mending Wall," Robert Frost wrote, "Something there is that doesn't love a wall." He and his neighbor built a wall between his apple orchard and the neighbor's pine grove. Pine cones would not eat apples, and apples had no interest in pine cones; so why was there a wall? His neighbor would only repeat what his father had said years ago: "Good fences make good neighbors," but his neighbor could not say why.

The apostle Paul and Robert Frost might have agreed that breaking "down the dividing wall of hostility" is the thing that makes good neighbors, not walls. Christ did that for us, and we must break down the walls that divide us from our neighbors.

PRAYER: O thou Prince of Peace, we thank you for breaking down the wall of hostility and guiding us to the way of peace. Amen.

Bruce E. Mills—King of Prussia, Pennsylvania

Luke 8:49–56   Give Her Something to Eat

THOUGHT FOR TODAY: But taking her by the hand he called, saying, "Child, arise." And her spirit returned, and she got up at once. Luke 8:54-55

The beloved daughter of Jairus died before Jesus reached his home. Even with this news Jesus encouraged them saying, "Do not fear; only believe, and she shall be well" (v. 50). Jesus gave her life again. It was a miracle. But then he instructed the parents to give her something to eat. Jesus could have given her food. On a grassy hillside, he had fed the five thousand with just five rolls and two fish. However, he gave this responsibility of providing nourishing food to the happy parents. Jesus and the parents working together restored and strengthened the little girl. There is much that we can do to maintain the life and health that Jesus gives.

PRAYER: Lord, there are many who need us to give them something to eat. May we be willing to share our food and the bread of life in your Word. Amen.   *Harriet Houston—Claremont, California*

Mark 14:3–9   The Personal Touch

THOUGHT FOR TODAY: For ye have the poor with you always . . . but me ye have not always. Mark 14:7 (King James Version)

A woman dared to do the unusual. She risked the chagrin of the guests to interrupt their dinner and anoint Jesus' head with expensive perfume.

Jesus defended her deed as more pertinent than feeding the poor. He announced his death again, but was anybody listening?

Few at that table were tuned in enough to Jesus to appreciate this woman's boldness or understand what it meant to Jesus. They didn't really see or hear Jesus as the woman did. She came straight to the point of his hurt in the only way she knew how—with a personal touch that meant far more to Jesus than even she realized. It won for her a place in the Gospel story.

PRAYER: Lord Jesus, make me sensitive to others' hurts and needs. Let me know when to give the hug, the phone call, or the personal touch that will minister love. In your name. Amen.

Pat Buysse—Derwood, Maryland

Genesis 2:4–9   Living Beings

THOUGHT FOR TODAY: "I came that they may have life, and have it abundantly." John 10:10

Kahlil Gibran has a picture of a handful of clay on the cover of one of his books. Out of the clay two figures—a man and a woman—are emerging. God is creating them and breathing into them the breath of life.

"Being" is one of Paul Tillich's favorite words. His classic book is called *The New Being.* The old being is Adam. The new being is Jesus Christ. Anyone who is "in Christ" is a new being.

New beings have a sense of destiny. New beings know the difference between good and evil. They are aware of death and dying. New beings can remember a faith past, enjoy living in faith in the present, and hope for a redeemed future.

In the beginning the Lord God made us living beings. Being is what you are: your soul, character, endurance, faith, and hope. Being is *you!*

PRAYER: Lord Jesus, give me meaning, give me purpose, give me direction. Amen.   *Richard L. Keach—Hartford, Connecticut*

Mark 4:35–41   Keep Rowing

THOUGHT FOR TODAY: Jesus will intervene when he is ready; we need to continue to row the boat patiently.

After teaching the multitudes, Jesus and the disciples boarded a small fishing boat to cross the Sea of Galilee. Jesus went to the stern of the boat and immediately fell asleep. A violent storm arose and filled the boat with dashing waves. The danger was great. The disciples fought against the storm while Jesus slept.

We, too, need to be "rowing the boat" for Jesus. He leaves to us the work of witnessing and spreading his word. But he is always with us in our "boat." No matter how hard the rowing becomes, Jesus is always there to help us. Jesus provides the strength to calm the crisis of life's sea.

Are you rowing in the strength of the Lord?

PRAYER: Lord, help us never to stop rowing when the winds blow against us. Help us to row in your strength! Amen.

Glenn A. Hamer—Petersburg, Indiana

Proverbs 31:10–31   In Praise of Mothers

THOUGHT FOR TODAY: Her children stand and bless her; so does her husband. Proverbs 31:28 *(The Living Bible)*

In the sixties, my friend John Roberts took a trip on a plane on which several sailors were returning from duty in Vietnam. As the plane landed, a man stepped from the crowd and approached one of the sailors, a tall, thin boy, hardly twenty, who shook his hand gravely, greeting him as "Pop."

Looking beyond his dad, the youth's eyes searched the crowd until he distinguished a shy little woman, a foot shorter than he, working her way toward him. He dropped his bag and swept her into his arms with a single word—"Mom!" She clung to her son for a long minute, pushed back for a good look, couldn't see him for the tears that spilled down her cheeks, and held him close again.

PRAYER: Thank you for our mothers, O God. Amen.

James H. Cox—Middletown, Kentucky

2 Corinthians 12:1–6   A Workman Approved

THOUGHT FOR TODAY: God is not served by technical incompetence. Dorothy L. Sayers

There is an old hymn which has certain words I always stumble over: "Would He devote that sacred head for such a worm as I?" I am a child of God, created in his image; I am not a worm!

To avoid the sin of pride, many people put on a false humility. True humility, the Bible teaches, is found in service to others and in refusing to set ourselves, as children of the Most High, above anyone else. Yet we are also admonished to love others as we love ourselves and to present ourselves as workmen who have no need to be ashamed.

General George Patton, never noted for his modesty, well knew his own capabilities. With disarming candor he prayed before a major battle, ". . . I am the best there is, but of myself I am not enough. Give us the victory, Lord." And the Lord did.

PRAYER: Lord, help me to be the best that I can be, knowing that by your help, success is possible without the loss of humility. In Jesus' name. Amen.   *Colleen C. Pearson—Salt Lake City, Utah*

Mark 10:13–16   Childlikeness

THOUGHT FOR TODAY: A childlike faith in God sees the invisible, believes the incredible, and receives the impossible.

As a pastor I try to minister not only to my congregation but also to my eight-year-old son. After he accepted Jesus as his personal Savior, he wanted to be baptized. I wasn't sure he fully understood what he had done, so I put him off.

In a special service in which people filled out cards requesting prayer, my son, unable to spell that well, had his mother fill out his card. It read, "I want to be baptized. God wants me to be baptized."

Ever since then it has amazed me how much children understand about God's love. It's beautiful the way God works in their lives. It is a shame that we often lose that simple understanding as we grow older. But thank God we can continually see it in the children around us. It helps keep our faith secure!

PRAYER: Dear Lord, help me keep a simple faith in you and your power. Amen.   *Glenn A. Hamer—West Baden Springs, Indiana*

Psalm 91:1–6   The Shadow of the Almighty

THOUGHT FOR TODAY: ". . . how often would I have gathered . . . even as a hen gathereth her chickens under her wings, and ye would not!" Matthew 23:37 (King James Version)

God's picture of himself as a great brooding hen is a strange one. It is startling to consider the majestic Creator of the universe in this undignified role. Yet what dignity is there in a baby born in a dusty, smelly stable? Or a tortured, naked man hanging on a public cross? When we consider how often God has laid aside his rightful dignity for us, it is sobering and humbling. When we refuse to abide under the shadow of those almighty wings, where the protection and peace are offered and promised, we grieve the heart of this caring and nurturing God. Our nervousness and worried unrest betray our lack of trust. It's time to hurry back with our fellow chickens where we belong—under the shadow! From there we can do all things his way and in his time.

PRAYER: O God, it is sad to realize how often we scurry around, trying to face our problems with our own strength. Forgive us and draw us back where we belong. Amen.

Elisabeth Buddington—East Longmeadow, Massachusetts

Psalm 119:9–15   The Force of Habit

THOUGHT FOR TODAY: Thy word have I hid in mine heart, that I might not sin against thee. Psalm 119:11 (King James Version)

I did it again today! For six years I have driven down Tenth Street as I travel to work. For two weeks, however, Tenth Street has been closed in one area for bridge repair. I left home, drove the usual route, and then had to detour around the missing bridge.

How many times in our lives do we find ourselves doing things just because we have always done them that way? Sometimes the Lord tries to show us a better way, but when we ignore his suggestions he is forced to erect a detour to keep us from going off the bridge.

If we are open to God's direction through time spent in prayer and Bible study, we will not miss God's gentle leading to try another route.

PRAYER: Lord, help me never to become so ingrained in my habits that I am not open to your change in direction for my life. Amen.

Marilyn Christmore—Topeka, Kansas

Psalm 91 Safety

THOUGHT FOR TODAY: He will cover you with his wings; you will be safe in his care. Psalm 91:4 *(Good News Bible)*

The eagle builds her nest high on the rocky cliffs. When the young bird is ready to fly, she pushes him out of the nest. She then spreads her powerful wings and flies under him. When he begins to falter, she catches him on her wings and carries him back to the nest and safety.

In Isaiah 40:31 we are told that "those who trust in the Lord for help will find their strength renewed. They will rise on wings like eagles; they will run and not get weary; they will walk and not grow weak."

As Christians, when we falter in our Christian life or are faced with a difficult situation, we need only to reach out in trust to God. As we place our hand in God's, our strength is renewed. We are safe in God's care.

PRAYER: Dear Lord, deepen our faith we pray. Thank you for the assurance that we are safe in your care. Amen.

Grayce Farris—Atchison, Kansas

72

Ephesians 4:29–32 Chimney Fire

THOUGHT FOR TODAY: If we live in the light . . . we have fellowship . . . and the blood of Jesus . . . purifies us from every sin. 1 John 1:7 *(Good News Bible)*

Smoke and flames poured out of our chimney. We watched from the street as firemen went inside to douse the fire in the fireplace. They sprayed water on the roof to prevent sparks from igniting. Before long, there was only a thin trail of smoke.

"The chimney must have been clogged with creosote," the fireman said. "You'll have to clean it more often."

We learned to do that. Our present chimney, connected to a wood-burning stove, gets cleaned once or twice a year.

That clogged chimney has been a symbol for me of the clutter of our lives. Possessions and too many commitments can clog our spiritual lives and rob us of time with God. A periodic cleaning out clears the way for closer fellowship. Honest searching through prayer shows what to throw out.

PRAYER: Dear God, show me anything that hinders close fellowship with you. In Jesus' name. Amen.

Eleanor P. Anderson—Beckley, West Virginia

Ecclesiastes 3:1–8   A Time for Healing

THOUGHT FOR TODAY: . . . a time to kill, and a time to heal; a time to break down, and a time to build up. . . . Ecclesiastes 3:3

Each spring I watch for the first tip of a crocus leaf to push its way up through the dirt. It speaks to me of the coming of warmer weather. Year after year my eager little crocuses get hit by a late frost and are nipped back, sometimes clear to the ground. However, the frost doesn't stop them. In a few days they are up again.

All my life I have battled the problem of getting hurt feelings too easily. I have tried to develop a hard shell, but sooner or later it cracks and falls apart, leaving me crushed. Instead of developing a tough crust on the outside, I'm trying to learn a lesson from the crocus. Yes, I may get nipped back to the ground, but I can send out new shoots and bloom anyway. Sometimes I whisper to myself, "Remember the crocus, remember the crocus."

PRAYER: Lord, please give me a crocus disposition that won't be crushed by frosty remarks or cold looks, but will spring back up to brighten my corner. For Jesus' sake. Amen.

Martha VanDam Kingsley—Green Lake, Wisconsin

Joel 2:20–27   Working for the Lord

THOUGHT FOR TODAY: "Then I will make up to you for the years That the swarming locust has eaten. . . ." Joel 2:25 *(New American Standard Bible)*

Aaron felt called to the mission field as a young man. In college he fell in love with an attractive coed from a wealthy family and married her. She refused to give up modern conveniences for a primitive life in a faraway land.

Two years ago, Aaron's wife died. He is on a mission field after retiring from his prosperous business.

No one works as hard as he does at the mission, and when a younger man tells him to slow down, he replies with a smile, "God is restoring to me the years the locust has eaten in a wasted life. I must be about my Father's business. I have so little time left to serve him."

PRAYER: Dear God, we thank you for your mercy and forgiveness when we do not do our best. In Jesus' name. Amen.

Claudia M. Higgins—Colorado Springs, Colorado

Ephesians 6:10–18 The Storm

THOUGHT FOR TODAY: ". . . he makes his sun rise on the evil and on the good, and sends rain on the just and on the unjust." Matthew 5:45

In the trailer we felt secure, protected from the driving rain. Even the close lightning and persistent thunder gave only brief moments of anxiety. Then the warnings came: "Tornado watch in effect." Fear set in! Where would we go? How could we know it was coming? What could we do to prepare? Should we pray? Pray what? That we should be spared? That God would send the tornado away?

But God does not work that way. Didn't Jesus say that God sends the rain on the just and unjust? Is it not more appropriate to pray that God might give us the courage to face the storm? It is the same with all of life's storms and difficulties!

PRAYER: O God, give us courage and strength and grant that we may grow in our faith as we ride out the storms of life.

Ron Evans—Eden, Ontario, Canada

Psalm 62:5–9 Support Systems

THOUGHT FOR TODAY: . . . lead thou me to the rock that is higher than I. Psalm 61:2

The distant muttering of thunder increased to a louder rumble. My dog, usually so brave, followed me around the house, eyes fixed on my face, tail dragging between his legs. His nervousness was comic; his faith that I could protect him from the storm was pathetic. Seeing his misplaced trust in my powers, I thought back to what I had noticed earlier in my garden. While weeding the peas, I saw that they had wound their tendrils around weeds and other pea plants instead of climbing the fence as they should. I had to coax each vine into its proper position.

How like us, I thought. We look for support to so many feeble props instead of almighty God. Prayer groups, pastors, friends, family—all are prone to change. They move, die, disappoint us. Only God is constant! Only God is a friend forever!

PRAYER: Lord, remind me that my faith must be built on the solid rock that is Christ. Help me to stand and to lean only on you. Amen.

Elisabeth Buddington—East Longmeadow, Massachusetts

Jeremiah 17:5–10

Search the Heart

THOUGHT FOR TODAY: "I the LORD search the mind and try the heart, to give to every man according to his ways. . . ." Jeremiah 17:10

We have all heard at one time or another that you cannot judge a book by its cover, but never was this proverb made so clear to me until I had the opportunity to see beyond the stern exterior of a nurse. I had known this person for years and had come to the definite opinion that she was very thick-skinned and uncaring. Yet reports came to me that whenever pain or hurt came to a patient, this nurse was there, not with just a pill but with a real concern for the person as an individual.

Whenever I see her now, I'm reminded that too many times we misjudge our neighbors because we really do not know their hearts. But God knows and rewards accordingly.

PRAYER: Lord, help me to look beyond the surface of lives and find there the true person. For Jesus' sake. Amen.

Lawrence L. Hoptry—Kingwood, West Virginia

Day 20

Matthew 7:1–5

Judge Not

THOUGHT FOR TODAY: Therefore let us not judge one another anymore. . . . Romans 14:13 *(New American Standard Bible)*

While vacationing at Disney World, I was amazed to see so many sunburned babies. My disgust showed in my stares. What kind of mother could let that happen? I would then self-righteously smear sunscreen lotion on my children. Positioning the baby in total shade, we spent hours in the motel pool. Later I discovered to my horror that the sun's rays had bounced off the concrete onto my baby. I was the not-so-proud mother of a sunburned baby!

That evening we returned to Disney World and a barrage of disgusted stares. Being on the receiving end was very humbling. No one listened as I tried to explain.

How often do we play the self-righteous role when we are only a set of circumstances away from being in the same situation? If only we could remember, "There go I, but for the grace of God."

PRAYER: Lord, help us not to judge others, for as we judge, so shall we be judged. Amen. *Marilyn Boydston—Lenexa, Kansas*

Psalm 46   Singing Through the Storms

THOUGHT FOR TODAY: What then shall we say to this? If God is for us, who is against us? Romans 8:31

When the alarm awakened us on that June morning, there was not yet any evidence of daylight. Indeed, something of a storm was under way. There were flashes of lightning accompanied by rolls of thunder and some rather strong gusts of wind. In addition, it had started to rain.

Of course there is nothing unusual about such an early morning storm in Missouri, but it was the singing of the robins in the midst of the darkness and storm that spoke to my soul. From all that could be heard or seen, there was nothing about which they should be singing. But my ears were not deceiving me. They continued their song and each note they sang spoke of faith in a loving God in whom we can trust in the midst of life's storms.

PRAYER: Lord, save us from fear when threatening events confront us. Make us strong in faith through Christ. Amen.

Robert R. Allen—Maryville, Missouri

Acts 2:1–12   Transmitters of the Good News

THOUGHT FOR TODAY: . . . each one heard them speaking in his own language. Acts 2:6

The "Centennial Message" that special Sunday morning at the First Chinese Baptist Church in Fresno, California was "transmitting the message of Jesus from one to another." I noticed a wireless headphone among the gray hairs of a woman in the seat ahead of me. She was hearing in Cantonese the same words of the service that I was hearing in English. The headphones were given as a memorial gift to the church for the people who come to worship and do not understand English. *How wonderful this electronic age is!* I thought. On second thought, *how wonderful that down through the ages God has been speaking to people of every nation in their own tongues.*

God speaks to us today to meet our individual need, and everyone can listen and understand God in his or her own language.

PRAYER: O God, I thank you that you have spoken down through the years. May I be your acceptable transmitter in word and action today. Amen.   *Lorna M. Holmes—McMinnville, Oregon*

Psalm 139:13–18   He Cares for Me

THOUGHT FOR TODAY: . . . the Lord is thinking about me right now! O my God, you are my helper. Psalm 40:17 *(The Living Bible)*

I was tangled in a web of despair. God seemed so far away. Tears trickled down my cheeks and spilled into my lap. "Oh, dear God, where are you?" I cried. "Why am I up one day and down the next?"

Many of us have felt that way. But thanks to God I am learning to be thankful even for those days when nothing is going right, when I feel discouraged and defeated. Why? Because God is showing me that God is faithful. God never fails to reach down and touch me exactly where I am hurting. God fills my void and my hurt.

PRAYER: Thank you, God, for the way you do not allow anything to separate me from your divine love. Amen.

Joanne Farrell—Grand Rapids, Michigan

Matthew 7:15–21   The Unspoken Witness

THOUGHT FOR TODAY: "Not every one who says to me 'Lord, Lord,' shall enter the kingdom of heaven, but he who does the will of my Father who is in heaven." Matthew 7:21

The guest of a family was a small girl who was totally deaf. As the dinner was about to be served, the father bowed his head and offered a short prayer of thanks for the food. The deaf girl, from a home where grace was not said, saw the father as his lips moved in prayer. She couldn't hear a word he said but she later told her girlfriend in the family that she "knew what he was doing."

That father witnessed to his Christian faith, not by unheard words, but by what he did, by what he was. For that deaf child it was not the spoken word but the *acted word* which reached her. In *The Story of Civilization,* Will Durant writes of "the eloquent silence of example." All Christians can achieve this eloquence even if they lack eloquence of speech. We are known by our fruits, without which our speech loses its influence.

PRAYER: Grant, dear Lord, that the testimony of our lives may match the testimony of our lips. Amen.

Thomas B. McDormand—Amherst, Nova Scotia, Canada

Psalm 98:4–8
 Join the Song

THOUGHT FOR TODAY: Make a joyful noise to the LORD, all the earth. . . . Psalm 98:4

I sat in front of two mothers at a school orchestra concert. Each one told the other that her child played "first chair" of their particular instrument. I thought of all the youngsters who didn't play "first chair"— those who weren't the best on their instrument. I wondered if first chair was a position whose elusiveness left them feeling like failures. I hoped not, because if it weren't for all of those who play their hearts out, whether they're first chair or last, there wouldn't be an orchestra. There would only be an ensemble or a chamber group. The full rich sound of an orchestra, or band, or chorus, or choir, or civilization requires the joyful noise of each of its members.

PRAYER: Lord, whatever my talents, whether great or small, help me to add them to the throng who joyfully praise you. Amen.

Barbara Pauley—Fairfield, Connecticut

John 8:3–11
 He Wrote in the Dust

THOUGHT FOR TODAY: There is a great need for compassion.

One day some years ago, when returning to work from lunch, I found myself in a crowd that blocked the pavement. The police had cornered a frightened girl in a blind alley. Some individuals had already taken sides, either taunting the girl or calling the police vile names.

She was soon "captured," fighting and yelling the whole time. I knew she should be apprehended, but my heart ached for this person and tears came into my eyes. I remembered the day Jesus came into my "alley" and led me out to freedom—not judgment!

Jesus said, "Neither do I condemn thee. . . ." (8:11, KJV) to a woman almost twenty centuries ago. He said to the crowd, "He that is without sin among you, let him first cast a stone at her" (8:7, KJV).

I wonder how Jesus would have handled this situation if he had been there in 1980, when a girl was picked up for shoplifting.

PRAYER: God, we thank you for blessed assurance! Help us to understand the difference between hard crime and human frailty. Make that distinction known in our lives and give us a double portion of compassion. In Jesus' name, amen. *Carl K. Garlin—Collingswood, New Jersey*

Psalm 142:1–7   Lonely?

THOUGHT FOR TODAY: The LORD upholdeth all that fall, and raiseth up all those that be bowed down. Psalm 145:14 (King James Version)

Loneliness is no respecter of age, ability, or social status. Teenagers may feel desperately alone while trying hard to be part of their crowd. Entertainers, rich and well-known, often write of their despair amidst the glitter of fame. Handicapped persons and the elderly wait for visits from friends or family. At some time, we all feel loneliness. This struggle is not unique to any of us. Jesus felt the sting of loneliness. His family misunderstood him; his disciples argued over places of power in his kingdom, denied him, and betrayed him. Perhaps knowing that God's Son understands what we are going through will help in lonely times. We can know that God has been there, too.

PRAYER: God, when I am lonely, make me aware of your presence, that I may find refuge in you. Amen.

Virginia Fortner—Prairie Village, Kansas

John 4:5–26   Where Is Your Messiah?

THOUGHT FOR TODAY: "I have come in order that you might have life—life in all its fullness." John 10:10 *(Good News Bible)*

Each member of the choir had a folder in which was kept the music for the coming weeks. Some of the choir members took their folders home between rehearsals, but as new music was added, the folders became increasingly cumbersome. When Handel's *Messiah* was handed out, it was just too bulky to put into the folders. One member of the choir said, "I took my folder home, but I left my *Messiah* at church."

Isn't that what often happens? We attend church on Sunday in order to renew our spiritual energy, but we leave our Messiah at church instead of taking him home with us. It is only as we acknowledge the presence of Christ wherever we are that we are able to experience the fullness of the life that he offers us.

PRAYER: Dear Lord, help me to share all of my days with you, that I may enjoy life in all its fullness. Amen.

Phyllis I. Northrup—Glen Falls, New York

Psalm 73   Reliance and Reassurance

THOUGHT FOR TODAY: . . . you hold me by my right hand . . . and afterward you will take me into glory. Psalm 73:23-24 (New International Version)

Have you experienced frustration with good intentions or the failure of high expectations? Asaph, the writer of Psalm 73, could empathize with you. But he had a confidence that helped him cope with the present and look towards the future. He realized that nothing could break his union with God. Even if what had transpired was the result of his going his own way and using his own power, God could correct that tendency. God would hold him by his right hand. Then he would only be freed to serve as God permitted; yet being held, he would have God's full support in all he did.

PRAYER: God, take my right hand. I want to rely on you now and in the future. Amen.   *Margie Theiss—Eureka, California*

John 15:1–7   Brighten Your Corner

THOUGHT FOR TODAY: "But even the hairs of your head are all numbered. . . . you are of more value than many sparrows." Matthew 10:30-31

I love the story about the celebration of V-J Day at the Los Angeles Coliseum at the end of World War II. Over 100,000 people came to witness a pageant to honor the city's war heroes.

Suddenly the pageant stopped, and the lights went out. A voice spoke in words to this effect, "You may think you are unimportant, that your job has no significance. But watch."

The speaker struck a match. The tiny flame could be seen by everyone. He then suggested that the audience do the same. As match after match was lighted, the audience gasped. The 100,000 pinpoints of light illuminated the entire stadium.

When I underestimate my little corner of earth and I feel that my influence is of no consequence, I need to broaden my vision and know how valuable I am in God's economy.

PRAYER: Without you I can do nothing, God. But remind me that, with others who also seek your guidance, I can change the world. In Jesus' name I pray. Amen.   *Shirley Pope Waite—Walla Walla, Washington*

2 Timothy 2:1–10   Miscarriages

THOUGHT FOR TODAY: Take your share of hardship, like a good soldier of Christ Jesus. 2 Timothy 2:3 *(New English Bible)*

When we were living in Thailand, a maroon bulb appeared on the banana tree, and we knew that a regime of bananas was about to grow. Miniature green fingers appeared, and with satisfaction we watched them grow bigger.

Then one day Annie came to me. "I have some bad news," she said, "The banana tree fell down."

Stunned, I went out to investigate. I found the tree lying on the ground, its half-grown bananas broken off. *This isn't fair,* I thought. Then I noticed something. Small green banana shoots were coming out of the ground around the base of the fallen tree. New trees were growing.

There are many miscarriages in life. But they rob us of our dreams only when we keep our eyes on the fallen tree rather than on the new shoots. When our dreams crash down around us, we will always find new seed that God has scattered in the storm.

PRAYER: O God, help me see the possibilities in any situation and be flexible enough to let you work in unexpected ways. Amen.

Dathene Stanley—Townshend, Vermont   81

JUNE

Philippians 4:4–9   Free to Be

THOUGHT FOR TODAY: . . . but be transformed by the renewal of your mind. . . . Romans 12:2

Three-year-old Daniel lay on his back on the bed, bent in the middle with his legs against the wall at a right angle to his body. "Mommy, look," he said. "I'm the letter *L.*"

In quiet aloneness, reflecting on a single image, his body took on the spontaneous posture of his favorite letter. A new thought pattern inspired his imagination, and he discovered that a three-year-old can be more than just a boy. The transformation released him from conformation. His body became a living letter *L.*

How exciting! The plans to which the renewed mind leads *become whatever God had in mind* when God created us. God constantly challenges our imaginations to move beyond the limitations of our present frame of mind, to adjust our posture to the Word, to contemplate the image of the Son, to *be* like Jesus.

PRAYER: Today, Lord, establish my thoughts upon the unbelievably magnificent creation that I am. In Jesus' name. Amen.

Wonda Layton—Lynnwood, Washington

82

1 Corinthians 1:18–25   Living by Mottoes

THOUGHT FOR TODAY: . . . Let us not become tired of doing good. . . . Galatians 6:9 *(Good News Bible)*

Mottoes about life are often a useful guide to our way of living: "Honesty is the best policy"; "Love thy neighbor"; "Put others first."

But sometimes they seem to backfire. Our honesty ruptures a friendship. Those we have loved hurt us. We forfeit something we need.

It is then that our focus must be on Christ who has taught us this way of life. Only when he is our reason for such a lifestyle can it have meaning. With God, right is always right and has positive meaning and eternal reward. We may be denied or suffer, but we also grow in stature and wisdom and peace. It was Christ's way. It must be ours, too.

PRAYER: Lord, help me to affirm that your way is the only way, whatever the cost, that I may rise as Christ rose. Amen.

Walter B. Wakeman—Jefferson, Maine

Proverbs 17:13–17 — Circles of Friendship

THOUGHT FOR TODAY: A faithful friend is a secure shelter; whoever finds one has found a treasure. Ecclesiasticus 6:14 *(The New English Bible)*

I was surprised when the new nurse returned to my room so soon after medications rounds. She walked to the window, her face evidencing some inner struggle. Then she turned to the array of get-well wishes outlining the mirror. She touched the one with the words of Ecclesiasticus 6:14. "That card really speaks to me," she said softly. "It does?" I asked. "Yes. A while back when my whole life just seemed to fall apart, a friend I had known my whole life, but hadn't seen in many years, came and helped me get through it all. But I wasn't there for her. She did so much for me—I just wish I could do something for her." "Perhaps someday you'll be the secure shelter for someone else," I said. "That's how friendship works."

PRAYER: Dear God, help us to be pebbles in the pools of life, sending ever-widening circles of love to others. Amen.

Mildred Schell—Dayton, Ohio

83

Jeremiah 18:1–6 — Realignment May Be Painful!

THOUGHT FOR TODAY: But now, O LORD, thou art our father; we are the clay, and thou art our potter; and we all are the work of thy hand. Isaiah 64:8 (King James Version)

During a visit to Nekursini Christian Hospital in India, I observed the setting and plastering of a young girl's broken arm. No anesthetic was given, so the pulling and bending that were needed to correct the position of the break were extremely painful. However, once the alignment was corrected and a cast was in place, the pain subsided and a smile replaced the tears.

Broken relationships, especially with our Lord, can be extremely painful, but when we allow him to bring us back into the cast of God's will for our lives, we are healed.

PRAYER: Dear Lord, make me sensitive to your will for my life and keep me molded in that cast. Amen.

David Weidman—Mussoorie, U.P., India

Isaiah 38:2–6   Does God Care When I Cry?

THOUGHT FOR TODAY: The Lord God sees *all* of our difficulties.

One night a friend of mine confessed that she had not cried since she was seven years old. I was shocked at this, as crying has always been a healthy release for me from inner tensions. She said that when she was a child, her father used to slap her or become infuriated when she cried. So she totally stopped crying for forty years.

Before I left her that night, I asked that she and I pray about this during the week. To be able to cry seemed to be a deep desire coming from her heart, and a great need.

Two weeks later she called to say that one night her tears started to flow. She was so very happy! She exclaimed that it felt wonderful! I could hear the joy in her voice.

PRAYER: Most loving God, make us aware of the inner heartaches of others as you are aware of ours. In Jesus' name. Amen.

Deanna M. Wong—San Francisco, California

84

Genesis 22:1–14   Loved Intensely

THOUGHT FOR TODAY: We know that in everything God works for good. . . . Romans 8:28

At 4:00 A.M. I found myself outside the delivery room anxiously awaiting the birth of a long-awaited child. The nurse reported we had a beautiful new boy. He had several observable birth defects.

At one moment we felt helpless to do anything, but willing to do everything we could to help Matthew, and we lived in anticipation of his growing to maturity. Little did we know that the birth defects would limit Matthew's life to just a few hours.

In those brief hours of Matthew's life, he taught us much about ourselves and the fabric we are made of. We learned the meaning of hope in the midst of overwhelming odds, to love intensely, and the meaning of "all things work for good." Without Matthew we would have never known our capacity to love a child.

PRAYER: Lord, in the midst of life's great sorrows, help us believe that "you will provide" and all things will work for good. In Jesus' name we pray. *Gary W. Wagner—Green Lake, Wisconsin*

John 1:1–9   One More Step

THOUGHT FOR TODAY: . . . "I am the light of the world; he who follows me will not walk in darkness, but will have the light of life." John 8:12

Lightning flashed, thunder was crashing, and strong gusts of wind shook the old building where our family had taken temporary lodging during our vacation. My children and I were gathered around a table with one small candle, for the lights had gone out. When the electricity came on again, I hurried downstairs to borrow another candle from the landlady. Suddenly a strong gust of wind blew through the open front door, accompanied by a violent clap of thunder. The lights promptly went out. Plunged into darkness, I turned and started to take a step. Just then the lights came on again, showing me that I was standing at the head of a steep flight of stairs.

Sometimes dramatically and sometimes quietly, Christ comes into our lives to light our way and save us from disastrous steps.

PRAYER: O Lord, light all of our steps, that we may walk in confidence and faith. In Jesus' name. Amen.

Elinor Warren—Philadelphia, Pennsylvania

——————————— Day 8 ———————————

Psalm 1:1–6   A Different Perspective

THOUGHT FOR TODAY: Love never ends. 1 Corinthians 13:8

A few months after moving to a small town, a woman complained to a neighbor about the poor service she received at the local drugstore. She hoped her newly made friend would repeat the complaint to the owner. The next time the new neighbor went to the drugstore, she was greeted with a big smile, and the druggist told her how happy he was to see her and her husband get settled. He then filled her order promptly.

Later the woman reported this miraculous change to her friend and asked, "I suppose you told the druggist how poor I thought the service was?" "Well, no," the woman said, "in fact, and I hope you don't mind, I told him that you were amazed at the way he had built up this well-run small-town drugstore."

PRAYER: O God, help us to speak and to live with appreciation and love, expectation and hope, for this kind of lifestyle works miracles. Amen.

Gary L. Reif—West Lafayette, Indiana

John 8:1–11 Friend of Sinners

THOUGHT FOR TODAY: For he knows our frame; he remembers that we are dust. Psalm 103:14

Public shame fell upon the woman taken in adultery as she was hauled into the temple court. People considered Zacchaeus nothing more than a prosperous outcast. Her townspeople spurned the Samaritan woman. Yet the Lord Jesus said to the adulteress, ". . . Neither do I condemn thee: go, and sin no more" (John 8:11, KJV). He spoke gently to Zacchaeus, "For the Son of man is come to seek and to save that which was lost" (Luke 19:10, KJV). He spent time in the heat of the day talking with the woman at the well. For these—and for you and me—Jesus gave his life on a hill outside the city's gates, that city over which he had wept.

PRAYER: Lord Jesus, teach us to be as compassionate to others as you are to us when we sin. In your name we pray. Amen.

Amelia C. Owens—Floral City, Florida

2 Kings 11:1–8 Haven from the Storm

THOUGHT FOR TODAY: When Athaliah the mother of Ahaziah saw that her son was dead, she proceeded to destroy the whole royal family. 2 Kings 11:1 (New International Version)

Standing at my bedroom window, I fixed my eyes on the ominous clouds hanging overhead.

My preschooler and I were in the house alone. Suddenly I felt alone. Then I realized I had someone with me: the One who controls the weather. Drawing my son close, I whispered, "God, I'm afraid. Please take care of us."

I felt as if a drapery dropped from the heavens and covered our home. Then I heard something roaring outside, but I could see nothing. In a few moments the roaring was gone.

Later that evening, we learned that a funnel cloud had passed over our area. When we investigated, we discovered that a tornado had touched down just a mile from our home.

Athaliah cut a path to Judah's throne with tornadic force and lived up to her pedigree as Jezebel's daughter. But God dropped a protective drapery around Joash, and a bedroom became his haven from the storm.

PRAYER: Cover me, God, with the drapery of your love through all of life's storms. In Jesus' name. Amen.

Sandra Brooks—Clinton, South Carolina

Psalm 31:14–16 — Words per Minute

THOUGHT FOR TODAY: My times are in thy hand. . . . Psalm 31:15

How many words per minute can you type or take shorthand? This is the important question asked of stenographers as they apply for secretarial positions. I can turn this around and ask myself, "How many words a minute can I speak?"

Recently while visiting with a friend, I said something critical about a mutual acquaintance. My friend, in turn, said something nice about the person of whom I had spoken. A few days later, this friend of mine had a severe, though not fatal, heart attack. I thought of her last words to me, which were so kind. The questions came to mind: "How many minutes do I have left to talk? Will my words be kind ones or critical?" All of us have only so many minutes—so many words per minute—in which to speak. How will we use them?

PRAYER: "Let the words of my mouth and the meditation of my heart be acceptable in thy sight, O LORD, my rock and my redeemer" (Psalm 19:14).

Lorna M. Holmes—McMinnville, Oregon

Hebrews 11:13–16 — Life's Web Suspended

THOUGHT FOR TODAY: "I am the Alpha and the Omega, the first and the last, the beginning and the end." Revelation 22:13

It was a late afternoon in the fall. The sun was beaming through the west window of the office. Suddenly a thin ray of light caught my eye. On investigation it proved to be the sunlight reflected on about eight inches of a spider web.

There it was, shining in the sun, calling for attention. It was not possible to see the strands above or below the web. The web seemed to hang in midair. Obviously it had to be suspended between two points, but all that could be seen was the short gleam of light.

Life, as we know it, is suspended between the Alpha and the Omega of God. We do not see God who is pure Spirit, but in faith we accept that from him we have come and to him shall we return. It is in the assurance of the faith that God upholds all of life that we live out our days.

PRAYER: O God, when life seems as frail and fragile as a web, help us to trust in you as the Alpha and Omega of all life. Amen.

Robert R. Allen—Maryville, Missouri

Joel 2:11–17   Putting the Pieces Together Again

THOUGHT FOR TODAY: "Yet even now," says the LORD, "return to me with all your heart. . . ." Joel 2:12

Made of meaningless fragments of glass, a window in Wells Cathedral, England, looks like a modern abstract painting. The story of it is intriguing. During the Reformation there was such revulsion against any stained glass window that portrayed God in human form that devout people went through the church breaking all windows showing God in physical shape. When their tempers had cooled, they gathered up the fragments and made this abstract window out of the pieces.

Joel was saying to a people long ago, "Even though you are broken and fragmented, God is *still* pouring out the Spirit on you who will believe." Out of a time of penitence comes a use of the broken pieces that brings joy out of suffering.

PRAYER: God, we come again to you. We rend our hearts. Help us to put the pieces together again. In Jesus' name. Amen.

Robert N. Zearfoss—Evanston, Illinois

Isaiah 58:6–11   Especially Blessed

THOUGHT FOR TODAY: Special blessings bring special responsibilities.

The early morning cold penetrated deep inside me as I watched a circle of barefooted, bare-armed children in Africa who stood around the flagpole. Many of them had not had breakfast, and some would have nothing at all to eat until that night around a campfire beside a hut. But their sweet voices rang out in praise as they sang the national anthem of their beloved country.

I thought of my own country—a land blessed with shoes and houses and food, a land of schools and hospitals and churches, a land of freedom and liberty and justice.

My eyes grew moist as I thought of another flag unfurled in another land. That flag represented so much to so many, and I was one of the fortunate ones to be a part of its blessings. I knew I was blessed!

PRAYER: Dear Lord, help us learn how to make our nation a blessing to all nations. For Jesus' sake. Amen.

Dathene Stanley—Townshend, Vermont

Ephesians 4:1–7   Open the Door

THOUGHT FOR TODAY: How wonderful it is, how pleasant, for God's people to live together in harmony! Psalm 133:1 *(Good News Bible)*

Most of us can remember this finger play from childhood: "Here's the church, and here's the steeple; Open the door and see all the people!"

When you open the door of your church, what kind of people do you see? Are there some who are jealous of one another? Are there exclusive cliques? Are the church members disloyal to one another through gossip and deceit? Can people disagree peaceably, or does a spirit of contention and bitterness develop?

A loving relationship between members of a church will promote a vital Christian testimony in the community. Let us check up on ourselves to see if we are doing all that we can to further a unified spirit in our local congregation.

PRAYER: Help me, God, to squelch bitterness and to spread harmony and love among my Christian brothers and sisters. For Jesus' sake. Amen.   *Shirley Myers—Zanesville, Ohio*

Hebrews 12:1–6   Conquerors

THOUGHT FOR TODAY: I can do all things in him who strengthens me. Philippians 4:13

Following his release from captivity by the Red Brigades terrorist group, General James Dozier spoke of certain people whose sustaining presence came to him vividly as they prayed for him.

Paul must have had a somewhat similar experience when he wrote, "Who shall separate us from the love of Christ? Shall tribulation, or distress, or persecution, or famine, or nakedness, or peril, or sword?" Then he gives us the answer, "No, in all these things we are more than conquerors through him who loved us" (Romans 8:35, 37). What comfort these words are to us, especially when we suffer a great loss.

The author of Hebrews says we are surrounded by "so great a cloud of witnesses" as he encourages us to run the race of life. Somehow we think of our departed loved ones and the great pioneers of faith, watching and cheering us on when we face "trials dark on every hand and we cannot understand." We do know that God's grace is sufficient.

PRAYER: Dear God, I need you every hour. Stay nearby. Amen.

Arlena Hasel—Cincinnati, Ohio

Luke 12:13–21   Let Go and Live!

THOUGHT FOR TODAY: " '. . . Then who will get all these things you have kept for yourself?' " Luke 12:20 *(Good News Bible)*

I like to build ship models. My problem is that of the many that I have put together I have nothing to show. The first model was wrecked by a suction-cup missile from a dart gun two hours after the model's appearance on the mantle. The second, after six months' work, was dropped down the stairs during spring cleaning. A third lasted six months until it was demolished by a football the children were tossing around the living room.

I have to say that the joy for me has been in the building. No one can take away all the hours of fun I had or the peace of mind and relaxation I felt. The joy and wonder of life does not come from gathering all the goodies together and saying, "Look what I've got!" It comes from living and doing.

PRAYER: Dear God, sometimes we think that holding onto things is the best way to live. Help us to see we live only by surrendering all that we are to you. Amen.   *Glenn C. Abbott—Sioux Falls, South Dakota*

90

Isaiah 30:15–21   Follow the Signs, Not the Crowd

THOUGHT FOR TODAY: Thy word is a lamp to guide my feet and a light on my path. . . . Psalm 119:105 *(New English Bible)*

It was our last night at the shore. We had just purchased a bag of caramelized popcorn and were looking for a place to sit quietly as a family and devour it. The rock jetty seemed perfect. Leaving the lights and noise of the boardwalk carnival, we walked to the rocks and sat crunching popcorn.

A dark shadow loomed behind us. We turned, startled, and faced a policeman. He told us we would have to leave and pointed to a sign. "Keep Off the Rocks," it said. We hadn't thought to look for a sign because we had seen other people sitting on the rocks.

How often, in our walk through life, do we follow the crowd and fail to look for the signs God gives to guide us?

PRAYER: Forgive us, dear God, when we ignore your signs. Help us when we stumble, and teach us to be alert as we walk through life together. In Jesus' name. Amen.

Francie Scott—Conshohocken, Pennsylvania

Luke 15:11–24   In Praise of Fathers

THOUGHT FOR TODAY: An old man's grandchildren are his crowning glory. A child's glory is his father. Proverbs 17:6 *(The Living Bible)*

A church school teacher told me of visiting a children's home with her fifth grade girls. They were attracted to a beautiful little girl about their own age.

"My four brothers and sisters live here, too," she said. "When our mother became an alcoholic, our daddy couldn't afford to keep us at home because he travels. Daddy was determined we wouldn't be split up so he arranged for us to come here. Daddy comes to see us every weekend and on our birthdays.

"But the time we look forward to most," the youngster added, her eyes twinkling, "is Christmas. Daddy saves his vacation for Christmas and rents a house for two weeks. We spend time together there—just the five of us and Daddy. It's the best time of all!"

PRAYER: Thank you for daddies who love us, O God, and who sacrifice to care for us. Help us express this to them. In Jesus' name. Amen.

James H. Cox—Middletown, Kentucky

Matthew 18:1–6   Love Those Kids

THOUGHT FOR TODAY: . . . Jesus said, "Let the children come to me and do not hinder them. . . ." Matthew 19:14

The people entered their small church and made their ways into their familiar pews. A very young, very shy little girl climbed up to sit beside her mother. In her arms the child clutched her teddy bear.

During the service, the child was so quiet that I had forgotten she was there, until I heard the bear. Out of habit, the child had pulled the string on the bear's back, and a sweet music box melody began to play.

The people neither laughed nor turned to scowl in disapproval. Even the mother did not hiss an embarrassed "Shh!" The congregation continued to worship, and the bear, after that one brief tune, was silent. These loving caring people are showing this youngster that God's house is a happy place to be.

PRAYER: Lord, help me remember to make your beloved little ones feel at home in the church. Amen.

Elizabeth Bjork Hill—Wilmington, Delaware

Psalm 107:23-32   The Lord Is There!

THOUGHT FOR TODAY: They that go down to the sea in ships. . . . These see the works of the LORD. . . . Psalm 107:23-24 (King James Version)

I once made a voyage by freighter to the Mediterranean seaports. The radio operator invited me to come to the "radio shack" each morning to listen to the daily news broadcasts from London.

One morning an SOS call came from the *Queen Elizabeth II*. The ship was drifting helplessly in the Caribbean Sea. The radio operators were friends and kept in touch as the repairs to the *QE-2* were made.

I came to understand that we were not alone in the vast ocean spaces. Other ships knew of our location, and we were aware of them. Through the miracle of communication, we were bound together into a fellowship of the sea.

PRAYER: O Lord of the earth, the sky, and the sea, keep me mindful of your presence wherever I may be. In Jesus' name. Amen.

Richard L. James—Williamston, North Carolina

Philippians 3:12-16   Brick by Brick

THOUGHT FOR TODAY: Only let us hold true to what we have attained. Philippians 3:16

I've always been impressed by this story of Thomas Carlyle. He had loaned philosopher John Stuart Mill his manuscript of *The French Revolution*. Mill's maid inadvertently used it to start a fire. When told, Carlyle alternated between rage and grief and settled into deep despair.

One day Carlyle saw bricklayers at work outside his window. "It came to me, that as they lay brick on brick, so could I lay word on word, sentence on sentence." So he began to rewrite *The French Revolution*, a classic in its field. It is a reminder of the kind of determination that can overcome tribulation.

PRAYER: Lord, when things go wrong, keep me aware that I can start each day's work anew with you. Amen.

Shirley Pope Waite—Walla Walla, Washington

Luke 6:31; 1 John 4:7–12   His Mysterious Ways

THOUGHT FOR TODAY: Smile! God loves you!

Teaching a teenage Sunday church school class for fifteen years was one of the most rewarding events of my life. I not only learned how young people felt about solving their own problems; I saw them reach out to encourage and inspire one another.

One Sunday morning a lady brought her grandson to our room, explaining that he would be spending the summer with her and would like to attend our class. As she turned to leave, her grandson reached out, touched her arm, and said in sign language, "Don't worry, I'll be fine."

Through his silent witness the young man taught the class a lesson about understanding and love. When he left us, the young people had learned the beauty of the words "Jesus is wonderful." We can learn from our youth about accepting others without question.

PRAYER: Our God, bless our youth today, and thank you for their outgoing and understanding love. Amen.

Viola Vanderpool—Gas City, Indiana

1 Samuel 3:2–10   Called by Name

THOUGHT FOR TODAY: . . . he calleth his own sheep by name. . . . John 10:3 (King James Version)

Jesus saith unto her, Mary . . . (John 20:16, KJV).

Jesus saith unto him, Thomas, because thou hast seen me, thou hast believed . . . (John 20:29, KJV).

. . . Jesus saith to Simon Peter, Simon, . . . lovest thou me more than these? . . . (John 21:15, KJV).

To Mary, Jesus' voice meant life as she mourned beside the open tomb. To Thomas, it conveyed light, for he doubted the reality of the resurrection. To Peter, it affirmed love that could mend his broken heart. To Adoniram Judson, it offered direction for work in Burma. To Dietrich Bonhoeffer, it gave the courage to live, write, and die for the glory of God.

PRAYER: Speak, Lord, for your servant heareth! Amen.

Henry Towes—Porterville, California

Psalm 46   Coping with Life

THOUGHT FOR TODAY: God is our shelter and strength. . . . So we will not be afraid, even if the earth is shaken. . . . Psalm 46:1-2 *(Good News Bible)*

Read the newspaper, and it is not difficult to imagine ourselves in the middle of a tornado, an avalanche, a war, or a cruel road accident or out of a job. On a personal level, sooner or later most of us find ourselves coping with an illness, caring for a sick relative, facing a surly neighbor or workmate, struggling to feel worthwhile, puzzling over a child who seems to be "off the rails," or grappling with the death of a loved one. When a child is late coming home, the telephone rings at a late hour, a telegram arrives, and events do not seem to add up, we fear the worst.

It is not just a matter of having to grit our teeth and bear it. Whatever happens today, God is here. God's presence and power are the greatest resources for which we could hope. We do not have to be afraid.

PRAYER: God, thank you that you are with me today. Calm me and enable me to face all things. In Jesus' name. Amen.

Richard Lawton—Adelaide, Australia

Habakkuk 3:12-19   A Glorious Optimist

THOUGHT FOR TODAY: . . . I will joy in the God of my salvation. Habakkuk 3:18

I have heard the preacher at the Park Street Church in Boston use Habakkuk 2:20 many times as he approached the pulpit on Sunday mornings. What a lovely way to begin a morning service! "The LORD, is in his holy temple; let all the earth keep silence before him." What a blessing would be ours if, instead of moving about and whispering, we would be quiet "before him"!

The prophet concludes his three short chapters with, "Although the fig-tree does not burgeon, the vines bear no fruit, the olive-crop fails, the orchards yield no food . . . there are no cattle in the stalls, yet I will exult in the LORD and rejoice in the God of my deliverance. The LORD God is my strength . . ." (Habakkuk 3:17, NEB).

PRAYER: God, enable us to trust you more fully and look to you only as did the prophet. In Jesus' name. Amen.

Theodore E. Bubeck—Lakewood, New Jersey

Jeremiah 31:31–34　　　　　　Trouble Remembering

THOUGHT FOR TODAY: ". . . I will forgive their iniquity, and I will remember their sin no more." Jeremiah 31:34

A headline in the newspaper caught my eye. I've cut it out and mounted it on my bulletin board. In large letters it reads: "Memory lapses not uncommon in aged; don't be terrified by them."

The article under the headline treated the problem psychologically; my problem is more practical. I'm just not as sharp as I once was. Smarter, maybe, but forgetful. It's reassuring to know that my condition is "par for the course." I'm normal!

There's another assurance that I need from time to time. I find it in the words of the prophet Jeremiah. He quotes the word of the Lord as it came to him: "I will remember their sin no more." God, too, is forgetful! Purposely forgetful!

PRAYER: Dear God, thank you for being forgetful when it comes to my sins! Teach me to be forgetful of the sins of others. Amen.

Raymond Jennings—King of Prussia, Pennsylvania

95

Psalm 90　　　　　　Ongoing Stream of Faith

THOUGHT FOR TODAY: The Christian faith is always only one generation away from extinction.

In the Oxford University Church of St. Mary the Virgin is a plaque that reads: "Christian worship has been conducted on this spot for the past nine hundred years." For almost half of the total span of the history of Christianity, God's praises have been sung, the Scriptures read, prayers offered, and the gospel preached in that one location. Think of all that this has meant in terms of loyalty, perseverance, and the passing on of the faith from one generation to another!

This reminds us of the ongoing stream of faith that is our religion. Year by year, century after century, Christians have contributed to that stream and kept it flowing. What about us? By our gifts of service, time, and money do we keep the stream of faith flowing in our church? In our homes do we do all that we can to keep our faith flowing?

PRAYER: God of the past, the present, and the future, help me to be a worthy part of the ongoing stream of the Christian faith. Amen.

Douglas W. Passage—Penn Yan, New York

Genesis 49:33–50:14   The Days of Weeping Are Past

THOUGHT FOR TODAY: The bird of sorrow may fly close, but it need not build a nest.

Jacob died and his son Joseph mourned. There was weeping for the forty days required for embalming, and then there was weeping for seventy days. Then the writer of Genesis states, ". . . the days of weeping for him were past . . ." (50:4). Not quite. Joseph took his father's body to Atad in Canaan, and there was sorrowful lamentation and mourning for seven more days.

We all have had or will have days of sorrow. No one is denying the need to mourn. However, you do not need to live in sorrow for the rest of your life. It's one thing to be nostalgic and recall the past—even unpleasant events—but you need not pitch your tent among the sorrowful ruins. There is a time to let go. The days of weeping are past.

PRAYER: God, there is a time to weep and a time to laugh. Help me in organizing my time so I expend more of my time laughing. Amen.

William W. McDermet III—Indianapolis, Indiana

Hebrews 11:32–40   Unrewarded Faith

THOUGHT FOR TODAY: And all these, though well attested by their faith, did not receive what was promised, since God had foreseen something better for us, and apart from us they should not be made perfect. Hebrews 11:39-40

Ours is an age of refugees. In Africa, Asia, even Europe and Latin America, millions of people are fleeing their homelands. I cried as I read the recent account of thirty-three Haitians who drowned in the surf fifty yards off the coast of Florida. Their frail boat had carried them within sight of their promised land. But of the sixty-seven persons aboard the twenty-five-foot boat, only thirty-four made it to shore. And *they* were to be returned to their homeland!

These folk set out in hope and faith, but that was not enough to save them. The fulfillment of their dreams was dependent upon others— upon people like us. It is too late for us to help the thirty-three now, but we can help others like them. God decrees our involvement!

PRAYER: Dear God, be a living, comforting presence to the homeless and distressed of the world. Be that presence in and through us. For Jesus' sake. Amen.   *Raymond Jennings—King of Prussia, Pennsylvania*

JULY

1 Peter 5:6–7; Galatians 6:2–5   Responding to Trouble

THOUGHT FOR TODAY: Immediately and later, the troubles no one would choose, God and people can use.

My beautifully iced angel food cake took on a new look in one second as I stepped from the car into my friends' yard. Obviously I had not secured the two parts of the cake carrier together, for there I stood with the top of the carrier in one hand, the bottom in the other, and the cake upside down on the lawn.

When a person's life turns unhappily upside down, there are at least two kinds of responses: The immediate—giving of self to God for a "redo" and considering the suggestions made by others; and the slower response—just plain helping one's self.

PRAYER: Thank you, God, that there's more than one way of responding to trouble. Give me wisdom as I try each way. Amen.

Lucille C. Turner—Frankfort, Indiana

————————— Day 2 —————————

Luke 8:22–25   The Power of Faith

THOUGHT FOR TODAY: Faith is to be ultimately concerned. Paul Tillich

This four-verse story in Luke says that Jesus had an undying faith in persons and asks others to consider the power of faith. The story begins with, "Let us go . . ."—Jesus was restless to reach people. Let us go into the cities to provide housing. Let us go to persons and speak to them about Jesus. Let our church go forward. Then a storm of wind came down the lake and the disciples were frightened.

The disciples awoke Jesus. He rebuked the waves and there was a calm. Jesus has power over the roaring elements of life. If God is for us, what "shall separate us from the love of Christ"? He said to them, "Where is your faith?"—faith means giving ourselves over to God so that we may discover the truth of being calm. Faith is asking and expecting to receive. Faith is seeking and expecting to find. Faith is "ultimate concern." Faith is a centered act of mind, heart, and will.

PRAYER: God! Give me faith as a mustard seed, faith so as to remove the mountains which stand before me. In Jesus' name. Amen.

Richard L. Keach—Hartford, Connecticut

Mark 3:7–12   Leaders and Followers

THOUGHT FOR TODAY: All these people came to Jesus because they had heard of the things he was doing. Mark 3:8 *(Good News Bible)*

When colleges were crowded and difficult to get into, a Christian girl filled out admittance forms for a nearby college. One question asked if she were a leader or a follower. She agonized over the question, thinking that she might be turned down if she answered truthfully, but her conscience forced her to admit that she was a follower. In due time she received a letter of acceptance with a handwritten message, "We think every college needs at least one follower."

Strong leaders are important, and God has used them many times to return people to righteous living. No matter how forceful a leader may be, he or she must have dedicated followers. God needs a few powerful leaders and a multitude of faithful followers.

PRAYER: Dear God, as a Christian follower, help me to be discerning about which leader I follow. Amen.   *Mary Jo Sanders—Lubbock, Texas*

Matthew 5:13–16   Salt of the Earth

THOUGHT FOR TODAY: "You are like salt for all mankind." Matthew 5:13 *(Good News Bible)*

We wound through the hills of West Virginia, searching for the right property. We didn't find it, but we did find a haunting beauty there in the hills.

As we left to go, the young real estate agent shook our hands warmly. "I came here because of the land," he told us, "but I stayed because of the people—they are even more wonderful than the land." I looked into his gentle blue eyes and believed him.

What a beautiful compliment! I went away thinking. Wouldn't it be wonderful if someone could say the same thing about each of us?

We tend to forget that a great nation cannot exist without great people. But we need to remember again and again until the whole world shakes its head in amazement and says about those of us who live in our hamlets and hills and cities, "They're even more wonderful than their land."

PRAYER: Dear God, help me be part of the strength of the nation I love so much. In Jesus' name. Amen.   *Dathene Stanley—Townshend, Vermont*

Esther 1:10–20   Declaring Your Rights

THOUGHT FOR TODAY: Declaring your rights is a gospel affirmation. Each person is loved and accepted by God.

Xerxes the Great held a celebration for his staff. On the seventh day he summoned his wife, Vashti, to parade before them. Vashti refused to obey the king's command. After her refusal to perform for his stag party, he banished her. This led to the selection of Esther as queen. I admire and respect Vashti. She affirmed her dignity and personhood.

How do we treat those near to us? Selfishly? With dignity and understanding? It wasn't easy or painless for Vashti to declare her rights. As Christians, we need to remind ourselves that there should not be dual standards; in God's sight all are equal. No person should be considered the property of someone else. No human should be stereotyped, categorized, or pigeon-holed.

PRAYER: Lord, we affirm that you love each of us with a richness and depth beyond our wildest imagination. Amen.

Arthur H. Kuehn—Lewiston, Maine

Psalm 8   For What Am I Searching?

THOUGHT FOR TODAY: My greatest discovery is to know who I am.

In a television movie that dramatized the life of David Copperfield, there is a scene in which David is standing on the eastern shore of England looking out into the sea near where his closest friend had drowned. With the wind blowing through his hair, he stands in deep thought, remembering the past. There is a flashback of voices from his childhood and of the many people he knew and loved, now gone from his life forever. In a moment of great nostalgia he throws his hands down and says, "What am I searching for? I must be searching for myself."

David the psalmist wrote an answer when he asked the question in Psalm 8:4–5, "What is man that thou art mindful of him, and the son of man that thou dost care for him? Yet thou has made him little less than God, and dost crown him with glory and honor."

PRAYER: Dear God, help me to know who I am so that I may give myself to you. In Jesus' name. Amen.

Bennett F. Hall—Winchester, Kentucky

Romans 12:9–21   The Power of Love

THOUGHT FOR TODAY: There is nothing love cannot face; there is no limit to its faith, its hope, and its endurance. 1 Corinthians 13:7 *(New English Bible)*

I gently pet Louie, and he purrs loudly. It was not always that way. When Louie came to my family's house a year ago, he growled and arched his back. He bared his teeth whenever we reached out to him. Often he scratched us, and he liked to slink away to a corner to sleep.

But a year of love has transformed Louie. He's a "people" cat, now. He prefers our company; he begs for our attention; and he graces our hearth with his lovely, yellow fur.

People sometimes growl and scratch, too. When others approach, they bare their teeth and reach out to strike. But love transforms. Even as God's love has changed us, so God's love in us and through us can change others. It may take time, but love *has* time!

PRAYER: Our God, help us to meet hostility with love and compassion, knowing that behind hostility lies hurt. In Jesus' name. Amen.

Dathene Stanley—Townshend, Vermont

Luke 18:16–17   The Gift of Love

THOUGHT FOR TODAY: Remember God's gift of love and his will that we love all people—even those who are different from us.

I was nervous, afraid something would go wrong. What if I were unable to handle it? I gained courage and walked through the classroom door. Eight three- and four-year-old mentally retarded children looked toward me. I thought to myself how horrible it is that something like this should happen to children. I felt so sorry for them.

As days passed, I no longer looked at the children to see misshapen faces or short stubby hands, but instead I saw true, never-ending love. They love so easily: a gentle kiss, a breathtaking hug, or sitting by my side. Now I think of Luke 18:16: "Suffer little children to come unto me . . . for of such is the kingdom of God" (KJV). Each one will always have a special gift from God, LOVE!

PRAYER: Help us each day, O Lord, to see your presence and love in everything around us. In Jesus' name. Amen.

Diana Jones—Bossier City, Lousiana

Hebrews 11:1–10   Adventure into the Unknown

THOUGHT FOR TODAY: By faith Abraham obeyed when he was called . . . and he went out, not knowing where he was to go. Hebrews 11:8

Our family likes to hike the trails of the Adirondack wilderness. There is much that a walk in the forest can teach us about life's journey. One truth is that life is an adventure into the unknown. Even if one reads the trail guidebook carefully, listens to others who have gone that way, and uses one's imagination, the reality is always something else.

So it is with life. We actually know little of what the future holds for us. We have to go forward each day in faith, just as Abraham did. Each individual has to face his or her difficulties personally; but we are not alone, because God is with us. It was this trust in God that enabled Abraham to accept the challenge to venture into the unknown. It is this trust that can make life a great adventure for us, too.

PRAYER: Help us, Good Shepherd, to face the unknown course of each day's existence with trust, for you are with us. Amen.

Douglas W. Passage—Penn Yan, New York

Philippians 1:3–11   The Limits of Love

THOUGHT FOR TODAY: . . . it is my prayer that your love may abound . . . with knowledge and all discernment. . . . Philippians 1:9

In Paul's letter to the church at Corinth he cites love as the greatest of all God's gifts; but here he says that even love has its limits. Love is not blind but is to grow along with "knowledge" and "discernment," and its purpose is to "approve what is excellent."

It is easy to become sentimental about love—to wear it as a pin or to sing "Love, love, love" or "What the world needs now is love, sweet love." But Paul warns that love is to be hardheaded, realistic, and practical in its results. Love is no mere sentiment or warm feeling around the heart; it is a way of life—a way that involves our intellect and will as well as our emotions. Love—as we have seen in the cross of Jesus—is active, risky, and effective. So it should be in us, his followers.

PRAYER: Lord, teach me today to use the best of my mind and will in the spirit of love. Amen.   *Rex Woods—Neenah, Wisconsin*

Luke 8:43–48   The Healing Power of Touch

THOUGHT FOR TODAY: "Some one touched me; for I perceive that power has gone forth from me." Luke 8:46

The idea that touch heals and blesses is an old one—as old as the Genesis account of Jacob deceiving his old, blind father, getting Isaac to touch him and bless him. Even later, Jacob's wrestling with the unseen adversary at the river Jabbok presents the idea of being touched, healed, and sent forth.

The woman in our story knows all that. "If I can just touch him, touch his garment, I will be made well." If Jesus would just touch us and heal our chronic diseases and heal our warring madness!

I led a service in a convalescent home. The people were brought in, looking depressed, sick, lonely, lost. I went through the service, never feeling I got in contact with anyone. At the end of the service, in a desperate attempt to reach out, I went to each person, taking his or her hand in mine and saying, "God bless you." Their faces lit up. They smiled. They came alive!

PRAYER: Lord Jesus, touch us so that we can touch others and help them to come alive. Amen.   *Richard L. Keach—Hartford, Connecticut*

Genesis 41:50–55   To Forgive Is to Forget

THOUGHT FOR TODAY: It is better to forget than to remember.

Too many people are carrying heavy burdens which sorely affect heart, mind, and nerves because they cannot forget something which happened to them even in childhood.

Joseph's brothers, through jealousy, sold him into slavery. This was a tragic thing to happen to a son loved so much by Jacob but hated by his brothers. Such a harrowing experience could have soured Joseph so much that the sweetness of life could have gone beyond redemption.

However, Joseph found the healing balm for the hard knocks of life in the ability to forget. "For . . . God has made me forget all my hardship . . ." (Genesis 41:51).

Joseph forgot by counting his blessings.

PRAYER: God of mercy, help us to walk on the sunny side of the street when the shadows would overtake us. In Christ's name. Amen.

William R. Spence—Lakewood, New Jersey

John 14:1–14   On Being Untroubled

THOUGHT FOR TODAY: "I will not leave you desolate; I will come to you." John 14:18

Job says, "Man is born to trouble as the sparks fly upward" (Job 5:7). Jesus said, "Let not your hearts be troubled. Believe in God, believe also in me" (John 14:1).

I asked a Bible study group, "What troubles you?" One member said, "I am troubled about the millions of starving, dying, sick people all over the world." Another said, "I am troubled that I won't get my Social Security in my old age."

Troubles can be self-centered. Troubles can be concern for someone else. Troubles can be extremely painful.

Jesus said, "Do not be worried or upset" (J. B. Phillips). He could have added, "God is our refuge and strength, a very present help in time of trouble."

PRAYER: God, do not leave us desolate. Come to us, for we know that nothing can separate us from your love in Jesus Christ our Lord. Amen.

Richard L. Keach—Hartford, Connecticut

1 Corinthians 13   Where There Is Love

THOUGHT FOR TODAY: Where love and compassion dwell, the peace of God is there.

Mildred was a little girl who once lived in our neighborhood and knew only how to love. She taught all of us the meaning of compassion.

Mentally retarded children have an advantage over their more capable peers, for they have learned no hate or bigotry. You see, these things are unnatural emotions; they have to be taught!

We all have learning disabilities of one sort or another—from the severely retarded to the highly educated who may not be "retarded" at all but have other problems that limit their learning processes: jealousy, selfishness, hate, or greed.

Mildred taught us how to love one another—one of our generation's greatest needs.

PRAYER: Our God, help us to remember that, whenever we stop long enough to help others less fortunate, the light of Christ will shine, illuminating the darkness. Amen.   *Viola Vanderpool—Gas City, Indiana*

Habakkuk 1:1–5   What a World!

THOUGHT FOR TODAY: . . . "How long, O LORD, must I call for help, but you do not listen?" Habakkuk 1:2 (New International Version)

Crime, attempted assassinations, and violence of every kind seem to be the order of the day. The three short chapters of the prophet Habakkuk seem especially appropriate for such a time as this. Neither the prophet nor we must ever feel that God does not hear.

To the prophet and to us comes the answer, "Look among the nations; wonder and be astounded. For I am doing a work in your days that you would not believe if told" (1:5).

In response the prophet concluded and asserted his faith in God even when everything seemed to be against him: "The fig tree does not blossom . . . nor fruit be on the vines . . . and the fields yield no food . . . yet will I rejoice in the God of my salvation" (3:17–19).

PRAYER: God, increase our faith in you, even when all else fails. For Jesus' sake we pray. Amen.   Theodore E. Bubeck—Lakewood, New Jersey

Psalm 66   With One Voice!

THOUGHT FOR TODAY: Sing to the Lord all the earth! Sing of his glorious name! Tell the world how wonderful he is. Psalm 66:1-2 (The Living Bible)

I am unique! God made me! I do not look like anyone else. My fingerprints are different. I am left-handed and my writing is unique. In fact, it is very difficult to read. My mind does not function the same as yours. No one possesses personality or disposition such as mine.

My heart cries out to God in a unique manner also. It does not cry out in the same words or with the same thoughts that you might express. I do not cry out to God with the same need. My desires differ from yours, too. Nevertheless, God understands me.

God created me! Will you try to understand me, too? Will you let me have that freedom?

We ought to allow one another the right to be unique. In this freedom let us praise God with one voice and rejoice together!

PRAYER: God, give all Christians the ability and understanding to accept one another and to praise you with one voice! Amen.

E. June Emmert—Lynnville, Iowa

Psalm 85:1–6   Revival in Our Midst

THOUGHT FOR TODAY: Revivals never come cheaply or accidentally.

One who lived long ago in a time of great spiritual as well as material and national need was Nehemiah. When he came back from captivity to help restore and rebuild the nation of the Jewish people, he declared his action: "Now it came about when I heard these words, I sat down and wept and mourned for days; and I was fasting and praying before the God of heaven" (Nehemiah 1:4, *New American Standard Bible*).

Nehemiah knew the need of renewal and restoration, but he did more than merely face the need—he responded by weeping, mourning, fasting, and praying for days before God. Nehemiah prayed and revival came. Here is the delivery room of genuine revival. Here is where the labor pains of godly concern result in the birth of revival. Are we willing to put forth that effort for revival?

PRAYER: God, revive us, and let that revival begin in me. In Jesus' name. Amen.   *Jack Naff—Hood River, Oregon*

106

Luke 4:16–30   A Dream That Will Not Die

THOUGHT FOR TODAY: ". . . to set at liberty those who are oppressed." Luke 4:18

In the synagogue one Sabbath Jesus read this passage: "I came to set at liberty those who are oppressed."

In the play *One Flew Over the Cuckoo's Nest,* we meet a group of oppressed men and women in a ward of a mental asylum. In the midst of a motley crew, including a silent Indian, a man building a bomb to blow up the place, and a human vegetable, comes Randal Patrick McMurphy. He is a laughing, together, sensuous young man who is posing as a psychopath to escape prison.

McMurphy becomes a therapist and Christ figure, healing the sick, preaching good news to the poor-in-mind, and helping the deaf and mute to hear and speak.

There is a terrible cost to setting the oppressed free. McMurphy is given shock treatments and finally a lobotomy. The prophet Amos faced social rejection; Jesus died on a cross; Martin Luther King Jr., was murdered.

PRAYER: Lord Jesus, do not let your dream to set free those who are oppressed die within me. For your sake I pray. Amen.

Richard Keach—Hartford, Connecticut

Revelation 21:1–8   The Glory of the Unsatisfied

THOUGHT FOR TODAY: The future belongs to those who are mentally and spiritually unsatisfied.

A woman sightseer in Washington, D.C., stepped from a taxi and saw, on the facade of a building, the inscription, "The Past Is Prologue." Turning to the driver she asked, "Do you know what those words mean?" The taxi driver replied, "Indeed I do, Ma'am. It means you ain't seen nothing yet."

Plato did not lay down his pen until he was eighty. Grandma Moses began her career as an artist when she was sixty-five. All suggest that fullness of life belongs to those who are eternally unsatisfied.

The best of life belongs to the thirsty, the unfulfilled, the unsatisfied—to those who never cease the quest. The Bible says, "See, I am making all things new! . . . I will give to the thirsty the springs of the Water of Life" (Revelation 21:5–6, *The Living Bible*).

To desire God, to want to grow, to reach out in life—this is the glory of the unsatisfied. Reach out to life in some new way today.

PRAYER: God, help us to reach out continually to new heights of spiritual attainment. Amen.   *Charles E. Comfort—Mt. Pleasant, Iowa*

Philippians 4:4–8   Rejoice! Smile!

THOUGHT FOR TODAY: Rejoice! Smile! We never know what these simple actions mean in the life of a friend or neighbor.

I recently read of a man who traveled around the world. He remarked, "A smile was the one thing the people of every country understood. So I smiled myself around the globe and made friends in every country—without using an interpreter."

I am sure we all have experienced some difficulty with communicating and have found a ready smile to be a real asset.

But do we use that ready smile as much as we should in our everyday life? A warm, friendly smile is appropriate in any situation. Somewhere I read this legend: "Good nature begets smiles, smiles beget friends, and friends are better than a fortune."

PRAYER FOR TODAY: O God, let this be a day of rejoicing. Let ready smiles bring joy to the hearts of many. In Jesus' name. Amen.

Erma Fajen MacFarlane—Columbia, Missouri

Luke 5:1–7 — The Other Side

THOUGHT FOR TODAY: "Trust and obey, for there's no other way To be happy in Jesus, but to trust and obey."

Any kind of change can be a very traumatic experience. All new sights and sounds, even smells can upset a person's entire outlook on life. As a pastor, I had expected to be moved to a new field of service sooner or later but when that time came, I found myself wanting to cling to the old familiar faces and arguing that I should be allowed a little more time.

In spite of every argument I could muster, I still heard the Spirit within my soul saying, "You are my servant, trust and obey." What I had wanted was some kind of physical or emotional security, a Linus blanket for the ministry. God wanted me to cast my net on the other side of the boat, to use my God-leased talents in a new area so that God might be served, not myself. When I let go of my "blanket," putting my trust in God, the way became clear and smooth. It still is!

PRAYER: God, ever teach me to obey your will for my life and stop seeking my own. In Jesus' name. Amen.

Lawrence L. Hoptry—Nitro, West Virginia

Psalm 121 — The Mountains Remind Us

THOUGHT FOR TODAY: We are guarded by God's power.

As I look out from my window to the Santa Catalina mountains, I see a formation that looks like a hand with an index finger pointing upward. It is as if the mountain beckons all who see to look upward into the heavens. The greater Splendor, the greater Power, is up there.

Looking at the mountains is awesome and inspiring. Much spiritual strength can be gained by gazing upon them. They are like fingers pointing upward, reminding us that help does not come from the mountains themselves but that ". . . help comes from the LORD who made heaven and earth" (Psalm 121:2).

The mountains stand as sentinels guarding the valleys and the plains below. They remind us that God is ever watching over us, preserving our souls as we walk through the dark valleys and the toilsome plains of life.

PRAYER: O God, who has created the beauty of mountains, remind us that you care about us and that you help us. In Jesus' name. Amen.

Edward K. Stratton—Tucson, Arizona

John 1:43–49 No Guile

THOUGHT FOR TODAY: If we confess our sins, He is faithful and righteous to forgive us our sins. . . . 1 John 1:9 *(New American Standard Bible)*

Every time I read that passage in John, I experience the same feeling. Jesus, upon seeing Nathanael approaching him, said, "Behold, an Israelite indeed, in whom is no guile!" I feel a great admiration for Nathanael at this point. What a good man he must have been!

Imagine if Jesus could say about me, "Here comes a woman from Claremont in whom there is no guile!" That would be the ultimate compliment he could bestow upon me. Yet because I have felt true contrition for my sins and have fervently asked God's forgiveness, I know God has erased my sins and does see me without guilt. How incredibly wonderful it is to know that my God forgives me! It seems incredible, but because God's Word says so, I know it is true.

PRAYER: Dear God, thank you, thank you for forgiving me so completely. May I forgive others as you forgive me. Amen.

V. Jewel Tilden—Claremont, California

Matthew 6:14–15 Forgiveness, a Necessity

THOUGHT FOR TODAY: Blessed are the merciful: for they shall obtain mercy. Matthew 5:7 (King James Version)

We met our friends at Bradley Field in Hartford, Connecticut, on a Sunday morning. Our chairs made a cozy circle in the center of the airport as they shared some of their experiences abroad.

At one point I asked Ken, since his six children were already grown, what advice he had for those of us still in the process of raising families. He thought for a moment and then said, "Yes! Teach them to forgive you for all the mistakes you will make in raising them!"

I have never forgotten these words, and as the years pass, their value increases. I have come to realize that forgiveness is as necessary to life as our daily bread.

PRAYER: God, show us effective ways of teaching forgiveness so that love and grace may flow. In Jesus' name.

Arlene MacDonald—Norwich, Connecticut

Romans 8:28–32   God Lives

THOUGHT FOR TODAY: He that spared not his own Son . . . shall
. . . also freely give us all things. Romans 8:32 (King James Version)

We arrived in Quebec City, Canada, after an all-night bus ride, and our
first thought was to find accommodations for our short stay there. The
price quoted by a well-known hotel was more than we could possibly
afford. As we stood in the street uncertain of our next move, a lady
approached and, hearing our problem, offered us the use of her home.
But since she lived five miles out of town, we had to refuse her kind
offer.

We then took a walk along the Promenade by the waterside and sat
down to rest beside an old gentleman who suggested that we try the
house of a widowed friend of his. She had converted her home into
apartments. We took his advice and found that it was exactly what we
needed and could afford.

When we call on God, we can expect to find God.

PRAYER: Dear God, we give thanks for your daily guidance and loving
care through Jesus Christ. Amen.   *Flo and Jim Gellan—Denver, Colorado*

Galatians 5:22–26   Hard-to-Grow Fruit

THOUGHT FOR TODAY: Keep in step with the Spirit. Galatians 5:25
(New International Version)

The fruit of the Spirit are a mark of the dedicated Christian. To have
love, joy, and peace is the deep desire of all of us. Not only do they set
us apart and show us to be positive people, they also make us feel good!

Not so popular are the other fruit—longsuffering, gentleness, goodness, meekness, and temperance or self-control. These come only with
struggle and practice and sometimes leave us with a sense of frustration
as we work to control our natural temperaments. As one doesn't become
a proficient musician without practice, neither does one become a fruit-
laden Christian without working at it.

A Christian without the spiritual fruits can be a real trial to other
Christians and a stumbling block to unbelievers. But what pleasure to
know one who displays the marks of the indwelling Spirit!

PRAYER: O God, help me today to nurture the fruits of the Spirit in
everything I do. In Jesus' name. Amen.

Walter B. Wakeman—Rockland, Maine

2 Thessalonians 1:3–12   Why Hurry?

THOUGHT FOR TODAY: For thus saith the Lord God, the Holy One of Israel; in returning and rest shall ye be saved. . . . Isaiah 30:15 (King James Version)

A popular and busy minister met a member of his congregation who was riding out to his ranch. The member wanted to visit. Instead, the minister told of a busy schedule, allowing no time to talk. The man shifted in his saddle and said, "Hurryin' big for little reasons is the best way I know of not to live at all."

People complain that life is rushing by too fast and getting more complicated by the day. We are expected to give some time to God every day if we expect to be restored and refreshed. A Welsh miner once said, "You can't put a fence around time that is gone."

PRAYER: God, let us not rush through life nor neglect to spend time in your presence. Amen.   *Chloe E. Kelly—Columbia, Missouri*

Numbers 14:1–12; 21:4–5   For Our Instruction

THOUGHT FOR TODAY: All scripture is inspired by God and profitable for teaching, for reproof, for correction, and for training in righteousness. . . . 2 Timothy 3:16

It had been one of the hardest winters of my life. I had lost my job; my stepmother had died; my father, who is very dear to me, was in a nursing home hundreds of miles away. I was also far from my children and grandchildren. I felt sorry for myself and complained to God daily.

While reading about the struggles of the Israelites in the book of Numbers, I found that they, too, had complained greatly. Despite God's marvelous deliverance of them from slavery and help all along the way, they complained about everything. God got tired of their griping and told Moses they would be wiped off the face of the earth and instead a great nation would be made from Moses' family. I thought, *Those crazy people. Couldn't they remember how God helped them in the past?*

Then it hit me. If all Scripture was "for teaching, for reproof, for correction, and for training in righteousness . . .," then this was recorded for the likes of me, also.

PRAYER: Dear God, forgive me for complaining. You have taken and are taking such good care of me and mine. Amen.

Martha VanDam Kingsley—Green Lake, Wisconsin

Psalm 113   Praise: The Instant "Glum" Remover

THOUGHT FOR TODAY: Plant a mustard seed of praise and see for yourself how it removes a mountain of "glum."

One of humanity's greatest ills today is depression. Because no one has been able to isolate the cause, no cure has been found. The most effective treatment known to the child of God is praise.

Praise automatically erases negative thinking and corrects negative attitudes. It is very hard to praise while we walk the valley of despair. "It's not human," we protest. "Why should I praise God when he allows me to suffer disappointment or illness or need or pain or great sorrow?"

Because in the midst of it all if we truly seek God, we can find God's hand of love ministering to us in countless ways. This, in turn, bolsters our faith. Faith, in turn, anticipates good things ahead bringing joy.

PRAYER: We praise you, God, for all the good things you have in store for us in this life and for eternity. In Jesus' name. Amen.

Jewell Abdallah—Monongahela, Pennsylvania

Psalm 23   Comfort During Anxiety

THOUGHT FOR TODAY: God is our refuge and strength, a very present help in trouble. Psalm 46:1

It had been a glorious, cloud-free dawn but now I was enduring the last few hours before open-heart surgery. In spite of the brightness outside, my room seemed very dark. I reached for my New Testament, *Good News for Modern Man,* but as I tried to concentrate, all I could think was, "Even when walking through the dark valley of death I will not be afraid . . ." (Psalm 23:4, *The Living Bible*).

Perhaps it wasn't just by chance these words were in my mind. During all my stormy medical history I'd always gone into the operating room repeating this beloved psalm and serenity would replace anxiety. I knew from experience that God *is* with me during the darkest hours. With that knowledge I was able to relax completely this time, also, and leave my fate in God's hands.

PRAYER: Dear God, we thank you for the peace and comfort you give us, especially in our most troubled hours. Amen.

Dorothy I. Neel—Winters, California

2 Timothy 1:1–7   The First Textbook

THOUGHT FOR TODAY: Train a child in the way he should go, and when he is old he will not turn from it. Proverbs 22:6 (New International Version)

A great-grandmother shares the following account of valuable instruction she received in her childhood.

"In our family of nine children, Mother took time out of her busy schedule to get us acquainted with the Word of God. She took each one of us separately, selected a portion of Scripture, and had us spell it out in the German alphabet. This she started at kindergarten age and continued until we were able to do our own reading. Only a few of the children learned to read knowledgeable German. However, the early teaching gave each one of us a hunger to continue to study the Bible."

PRAYER: Thank you, God, for dedicated mothers who take time out of a busy schedule to teach your Word to their children.

Etta Gingrich—Lititz, Pennsylvania

AUGUST

Mark 13:33–37   A New Start

THOUGHT FOR TODAY: "Watch and pray . . . the spirit indeed is willing, but the flesh is weak." Matthew 26:41 (King James Version)

Today is the first day of a new month. As I made the rounds this morning, turning over the leaves on the various calendars, it was hard to believe another month had ended.

Although New Year's Day is traditionally set aside for new resolutions, the beginning of each month is also an excellent time, with God's help, to try harder to eliminate some of our faults. It is a time for thanking God for having given us another month of life.

But each day is really a day for new beginnings. Each precious day of life is a gift from God, and it should be lived *for* God.

So as we begin each new month, each new week, and each new day, let us strive to live it in a way pleasing to God.

PRAYER: God, keep us ever watchful, for we know not the hour or the day of your coming. In Jesus' name, Amen.

Erma Fajen MacFarlane—Columbia, Missouri

1 Corinthians 12:12–27   Belonging

THOUGHT FOR TODAY: Yes, the body has many parts, not just one part. 1 Corinthians 12:14 *(The Living Bible)*

A term that is significant in the fields of sociology and psychology is also meaningful in the field of computer technology: "integration." It is tragic when one does not have an integrated personality. How sad that in our global village we are not integrated. We all have the right to belong to someone or a support group or family.

A nameless, abandoned, deaf-mute Alaskan boy cried and walked for nineteen years, living like an animal in drain pipes and abandoned cars. He had no birth certificate and no Social Security number, and therefore he was ineligible for aid. However, in Los Angeles in December 1982, Virginia McKinney adopted him and saw that he was named and given a birth certificate. She said, "He has a right to be part of a family."

PRAYER: O God, thank you that I am part of your family and that some of the other parts care for me. Amen.

J. Lester Harnish—Lake Oswego, Oregon

Luke 4:16–21   A Fiery Sermon

THOUGHT FOR TODAY: "For the Son of man is lord of the sabbath."
Matthew 12:8

A church member who had been attending regularly suddenly stopped going. After some weeks the minister decided to visit his absent parishioner. It was a chilly evening, and the minister found the man at home alone, sitting before a blazing fire.

Guessing the reason for his minister's visit, the man welcomed him, led him to a big chair by the fireplace, and waited. The minister made himself comfortable and said nothing. Then, in grave silence, the minister took the fire tongs, carefully picked up a brightly burning ember, and placed it to one side of the hearth. Then he sat back again in silence.

As the lone ember's flame diminished, there was a momentary glow, and then its fire was no more. As the minister rose to leave, his host said, "Thank you for your fiery sermon. I'll be at church next Sunday."

PRAYER: We give thanks this day, O God, for the Body of Christ, the fellowship of believers, the church of which we are a part. Amen.

Gary L. Reif—West Lafayette, Indiana

115

Matthew 5:43–48   The Dog Who Preached a Sermon

THOUGHT FOR TODAY: To return good for good is human, but to return good for evil is Christlike.

Jesus told his followers to forgive those who misused them. Since the custom was to slap the face of an enemy, Jesus shocked people when he said to turn the other cheek.

Sir Walter Scott once threw a rock at a stray dog to chase it away. His throw was stronger than he meant it to be. He hit the dog, breaking its leg. Instead of running, the dog limped up to him and licked his hand. Sir Walter Scott said, "That day I clearly understood Jesus' words, as that dog preached the Sermon on the Mount to me."

The world needs to see a likeness of Jesus in every believer. With God's love, we can replace anger with love, grudges with forgiveness, becoming living examples of God's Word.

PRAYER: Lord, in our daily lives and service, let us be true disciples, showing love for Jesus' sake. Amen.   *Robin Lewallen—Mentor, Ohio*

2 Corinthians 5:16–21   "Cleanable" Lives

THOUGHT FOR TODAY: In what areas of my life do I need forgiveness?

When my children were toddlers, they started to help me in the kitchen by measuring, pouring, and mixing. No matter what their ages, they were always messy! One day after a big spill on himself and the counter, my son said, "We can just wash me up."

I smiled and later pondered how many times Jesus had "washed me up" spiritually. He had cleansed me of my mistakes, failures, and sins and had given me a fresh start each day. Because of God's love for us, we can live forgiven, "cleanable" lives.

PRAYER: Dear God, thank you for your forgiveness. Help us to pass on that forgiveness to others. In Jesus' name. Amen.

Carol Hegberg—DeKalb, Illinois

Hebrews 12:1–6   For the Gold

THOUGHT FOR TODAY: Let us keep our eyes fixed on Jesus, on whom our faith depends from beginning to end. . . . Hebrews 12:2 *(Good News Bible)*

How exciting it was to watch our men's gymnastics team win the Gold, when no one thought they would. Time and again we have been overwhelmed at seeing the victory of the underdog. Certainly the victory of that athlete who comes from behind is an inspiration to those who must compete after him or her.

In our lives we too often find ourselves behind, or at least overwhelmed by the competition. Our "underdog" feeling is often our defeat—but consider the victory of Jesus. Jesus was completely defeated: he was humiliated, beaten, crucified, dead, and buried. Yet, Jesus rose from the dead and won the Gold in spite of the odds, and because he did it, we also are inspired to do it.

Let's run for the Gold promised by God through Jesus Christ.

PRAYER: Dear God, help me in this game called life, that I may win the Gold through Jesus and defeat the competition of evil. Amen.

Duane H. Kincaid—Filer, Idaho

Psalm 23   Bought With a Price

THOUGHT FOR TODAY: Life has loveliness to sell, All beautiful and splendid things. Sara Teasdale

The French artist Millet and his wife stood looking at his hastily painted picture. "It is not very good," said his wife.

"No," replied Millet, "but we have to eat."

"Rather we shall starve," answered the painter's wife.

From that point, Millet learned the meaning of hunger and went on to paint his immortal canvas, "The Gleaners."

Achievements do not come by doing second-rate work. The deep meanings of our worship services grow out of heartaches, sorrows, and triumphs. The rights and liberties of our democratic civilization were bought with sacrifices beyond our comprehension.

PRAYER: Our God, make clear your purpose for us this day. Grant us to see by faith that which is withheld from our eyes. Amen.

Raymond M. Veh—Thiensville, Wisconsin

1 Corinthians 15:51–58   Alleluia

THOUGHT FOR TODAY: Every life has meaning.

While on a trip to Spain, our journey took us to the Valley of the Fallen, a memorial to the Spanish Civil War dead from both sides. It is a most impressive monument near Escorial, which was cut out of the side of a granite mountain. In the huge basilica is a mausoleum where eighty thousand men in lead coffins are buried. Forty thousand have no names. While I stood in the mausoleum, where there is a musty smell of death, a great sadness came over me.

As we came back into the vaulted-ceiling basilica, our tour guide told of a choir of young people from Ohio who asked, after visiting the mausoleum, for the privilege of singing in the basilica. Softly they began to sing, with the volume increasing as they sang, "Alleluia, Alleluia, Alleluia, Alleluia." They filled the basilica with their song. As I heard the story, I turned away from the group and began singing under my breath the song that so moved those who heard it. The gloom left me, and a feeling of peace and the presence of God filled my heart.

PRAYER: Dear God, thank you for the death and resurrection of your Son Jesus for victory over the meaninglessness of death. Alleluia! Amen.

Bennett F. Hall—Winchester, Kentucky

Genesis 1:26–31   If We Fail?

THOUGHT FOR TODAY: God said, "Let us make man in our image ... let them have dominion . . . over all the earth. . . ." Genesis 1:26

The retreat leader knelt beside the boy with Down's syndrome, listening attentively as the boy struggled to express his fears. "B-b-bu' wha' if people don' do wha' God wa-wants us to?" he stammered. Tears flowed freely as he struggled with the questions the youth retreat had raised: how dependent, independent, or interdependent are we? Do we need God? Does God need us? Do we need each other? In a world filled with war and rumors of war, our youth are afraid at each new crisis, but these fears are seldom expressed so openly. Now, as 140 youth and adults silently watched and listened, this youth expressed those fears.

Yes, I thought, *we were created for fellowship with God, and as caretakers of God's universe. What if we fail?*

PRAYER: God, help us to do your will here on earth. Give us wisdom to make our world a better place. Amen.

Lois E. Woods—Sumner, Washington

Hebrews 12:5–11   A Fruitful Experience

THOUGHT FOR TODAY: It is for discipline that you have to endure. . . . Hebrews 12:7

One morning as I was preparing a grapefruit, my thoughts were concerned with an unpleasant happening of the day before. Although I had the strong feeling that the experience was for my personal discipline and that good would come from it, my wounded pride had kept me from seeing the brighter side.

Upon taking a bite of the fruit, I noticed that the membrane which clung to it was slightly bitter to the taste. Yet I had been told that this very membrane, if thoroughly chewed before swallowing, was beneficial for its fiber content. "We have to take the bitter with the sweet," I reasoned to myself. After reading the passage from today's Scripture, I resolved to benefit from my recent experience. And somehow, the rest of the grapefruit tasted extra good!

PRAYER: Thank you, loving God, for those blessings which sometimes come disguised as unpleasant happenings. In Jesus' name. Amen.

Mary Hamlett Goodman—Dallas, Texas

1 Thessalonians 4:13–18   His Comforting Touch

THOUGHT FOR TODAY: God often uses little children with their simple, honest faith to give us words of encouragement.

How do you comfort a four-year-old whose friend has been killed? I knelt and held my grandson, as I struggled to contain my own grief and shock and to comfort him. Over and over I had to explain to him that he wouldn't get to play with Joey anymore. We talked about the beauties of heaven and how much fun Joey would have skipping along with Jesus.

I did a lot of praying that day. My grandson's little mind was struggling to find answers to his first experience of grief. I asked God to help me comfort him with the right words.

As I tucked him in bed, my grandson asked again where Joey was. When I said Joey was with Jesus, he whispered, "If Joey is with Jesus, will he hear me say my prayers?" As I nodded yes, he sighed and said, "That's all I need to know."

PRAYER: God, give us the simplicity of little children who trust you with every burden and heartache. In Jesus' name. Amen.

Mary Lou Bardill—Seymour, Tennessee

Matthew 6:25–34   What, Me Worry?

THOUGHT FOR TODAY: Worry is stewing without doing. It is interest paid on trouble, which never comes due.

Do you worry? If you are like most people, you probably do. Worry causes anxiety, ulcers, hypertension, cramps, headaches, and more.

Our worrying can be healed if we open ourselves fully to Christ and his words. The principle is to take reasonable care and then face life trusting and accepting each day freshly, leaving the unknown future in God's hands.

There is no magic formula for not worrying. Christ tells us simply to "trust in God." How? We learn to trust by trusting. This way we can stop relying on worry and begin relying on God.

PRAYER: God, help me to stop worrying about the unchangeable and start relying on your ability to take care of my life. Amen.

Glenn A. Hamer—West Baden Springs, Indiana

Ephesians 4:1–7   Repair

THOUGHT FOR TODAY: Do your best to preserve the unity which the Spirit gives by means of the peace that binds you together. Ephesians 4:3 *(Good News Bible)*

Fearing a big repair job with expensive complications, I finally took my ailing car into the shop. What a relief when the mechanic had only to flip a switch I had overlooked in order to solve the problem.

Sometimes there is a complication in a relationship with another person that needs a repair job. Often all that is needed is a simple word or phrase—"I'm sorry," or "I really care," or the simple action of a gentle touch, a thoughtful smile, a knowing nod. How simple the message: "God loves you and I love you." What a remedy it is!

PRAYER: God, sometimes I fear the worst and from the small problem make a large one. Help me to see myself and others in the light of your love. In Jesus' name. Amen.   *Freda Briggs—El Dorado, Kansas*

Exodus 3:1–10   The Lure of the Unexpected

THOUGHT FOR TODAY: One day while Moses was taking care of the sheep and goats . . . there the angel of the LORD appeared to him. . . . Exodus 3:1-2 *(Good News Bible)*

Does anything give life more zest than the lure of the unexpected? The big trees of California were discovered by a deer hunter. He was not looking for forest monarchs several hundred feet high, but he thrilled at the sight of them.

The daily routine of a shepherd's life at the edge of a desert offered little that was unusual. One day Moses faced an unexpected "strange sight" when suddenly he noticed a bush burning, yet unconsumed. Because of that experience he was soon back in Egypt to lead his people out of slavery. Abraham went forth "not knowing." He became the father of a nation. Sometimes the unusual is there but unnoticed. John Burroughs said, "Would you see something beautiful today? Then take the same walk you took yesterday."

PRAYER: O God, help us to live today with open minds and ready hearts. We pray in Jesus' name. Amen.

Charles E. Comfort—Mt. Pleasant, Iowa

1 Corinthians 15:20–28   Did the Birds Sing?

THOUGHT FOR TODAY: Good Friday is good because it reminds us of God's power of redemption which is part of God's plan of salvation.

It was dawn on Good Friday morning. The ecumenical breakfast for men had focused on the sobering events of the crucifixion of Jesus. As I swung the car into the drive, my mood was somber—perhaps sad.

But on the brief journey from the car to the house there came from the distance the beautiful song of a cardinal. At first I wanted to say, "Hush, don't you know what day this is?" Yet the cheery notes continued to fill the morning's crisp air. It was then that I realized the faith called forth by the song of that bird.

The bird's song came as a new assurance that the cross did not have the final word. Death is not victorious. God uses even death to bring about good and salvation.

PRAYER: Teach us, Lord, to listen for your messages of faith, and renew our hope that all things are used of you for good. Amen.

Robert R. Allen—Maryville, Missouri

121

Matthew 11:25–30   "Let Go and Let God"

THOUGHT FOR TODAY: Cast all your anxieties on him, for he cares about you. 1 Peter 5:7

Whenever one of my cassette tapes breaks, I take it to a friend who repairs tapes as a hobby. Last winter I kept telling my friend I had a tape to be repaired, but every time I went to her home I would forget to leave it.

At one point I thought I had left it, and I wondered why she had not returned it. In feigned desperation I asked, *"Are you ever going to fix my tape?"* My friend replied, "You brought that tape here many times, but never left it so I could repair it!"

That incident reminds me of the times I take something to God expecting to have it fixed. Without realizing it, I take it back, start worrying again, and then wonder why God hasn't fixed it yet.

PRAYER: Dear God, help me to remember that when I am worrying I am not trusting in you. Enable me to trust you enough to take my burdens to you and leave them with you until they are repaired. In Jesus' name. Amen.   *Sandi Cleary—Northfield, New Jersey*

Psalm 74:12–17   Then Comes Spring

THOUGHT FOR TODAY: . . . thou hast prepared the light and the sun. . . . thou hast made summer and winter. Psalm 74:16–17 (King James Version)

In the fall the seeds die. They are covered with leaves, and the rain brings water. Blinding snows cover them to maintain the warmth of the earth. Then comes the spring, and the seeds put forth a beautiful and precious new growth.

Winter also comes to the soul. Blinding discouragements and piercing adversities hover around us. We shiver from the cold; our feelings want to tell us that we are separated and apart from our God.

But God is not away. God tries, tests, and teaches us during winter, but then comes spring. A new growth spurts from within us. New insights and understandings are added to our spiritual growth.

PRAYER: God, increase my wisdom of you even if the cold winter seems to overwhelm me. Amen.   *Alice Gough—Media, Pennsylvania*

———————————— Day 18 ————————————

Genesis 9:12–17   Rainbows of Love

THOUGHT FOR TODAY: In this is love, not that we loved God, but that He loved us and sent His Son to be the propitiation for our sins. 1 John 4:10 (New American Standard Bible)

One day my husband and oldest daughter were watching a thunderstorm in the area. It was clearing and they excitedly started looking for a rainbow.

We learn about rainbows in Genesis. The rainbow is a sign of a covenant that God made with Noah. In Genesis 9:12–17, God tells Noah that the rainbow will remind him that God will never again flood the earth in order to destroy all living things.

The cross is like Noah's rainbow. It is a sign that God sent Christ in order that we might not be condemned, but instead we might have everlasting life with Christ.

God has given us many gifts and promises. When we see a rainbow or a cross, let us remember God's love.

PRAYER: We praise you, God, for your gifts of love which are ours through the cross of your Son. Amen.

Marilyn Reynolds—Georgia, Vermont

Hebrews 9:24; 10:19; 13:3–15   Where Is Your Sanctuary?

THOUGHT FOR TODAY: . . . He shall become a sanctuary. . . . Isaiah 8:14 (New American Standard Bible)

Last February our family of four went to the Philippines. We shared crowded facilities and found it difficult to find a quiet place for personal devotions.

How do Filipino Christians get alone with God? One pastor and his family of five live in a one-room "nipa" house. He sits at a table, quiets his heart and mind, and thinks of God. A student shared, "When I have my devotions, I put my covers over my head and pray."

In Hebrews we read that Christ, as our high priest, offered himself as a sacrifice so that we can enter into the holy place where God is. We can commune with Christ because he is our sanctuary.

PRAYER: Dear God, thank you for being present always, meeting me wherever I am. Amen.   *Barbara J. Hibschman—Vineland, New Jersey*

Proverbs 13:24; 19:18; 22:15; 23:13–14; 29:15   Train Up a Child

THOUGHT FOR TODAY: Train up a child in the way he should go, and when he is old, he will not depart from it. Proverbs 22:6

Years ago I heard a speaker tell this story:

Observing some children playing ball, a welfare worker noticed a badly crippled lad sitting on the sidelines. She was told he was run over by a car while playing ball in the street. Because his family had no money, the child was not taken to a hospital.

The welfare worker engaged a prominent doctor to mend the boy's leg free of charge and a leading businessman to pay the hospital bill. The bone was rebroken and properly set. In a short while, the boy was running, laughing, and playing ball again.

"Would you like to know where he is now?" the speaker asked. "He's in the state penitentiary. The welfare worker was so busy helping him learn *how* to walk she forgot to teach him *where* to walk."

PRAYER: Guide us where you want us to go, dear Lord, and gave us wisdom in instructing the children entrusted to us. Amen.

James H. Cox—Middletown, Kentucky

Matthew 9:21–22   A Child's Faith

THOUGHT FOR TODAY: . . . for she said to herself, "If I only touch his garment, I shall be made well." Matthew 9:21

My husband had been ill for some time, and the whole family was much concerned. Our small grandson, Tyson, was spending the day with us. Tyson said, "Grandma, remember when we went to see the picture show *ET*?" "Yes," I said. Tyson continued, "Do you remember how ET touched things with his finger and made them all well? Wouldn't it be wonderful if ET could touch Grandpa and make him all well again?" O to have the faith of a small child!

I was reminded of the story in the Bible of the woman who had been ill for twelve years. All she did was touch the fringe of Jesus' garment and Jesus made her well. Jesus said, "Take heart, daughter, your faith has made you well."

PRAYER: Dear God, give us the faith of a little child when we ask for your help. In Jesus' name. Amen.

Emily B. Holcomb—Broken Bow, Nebraska

Psalm 100   Time Out

THOUGHT FOR TODAY: An enforced pause can give new insights.

On the last day of the month we had a terrific rainstorm with thunder and lightning. The next morning I learned that the lightning had put the bank's main computer out of commission. Our annuity had not been posted. This meant I could not shop for staples, or do the other first-of-the-month errands. It also gave me time to think.

What if my husband and I still had a large family to feed and there was no money coming in? My husband has health problems, and a granddaughter just had knee surgery—what if we could not afford medical care or lived where there was none available? What if we had no comfortable home?

I used some of my free time to thank God for these things, and I promised to do more for those who are less fortunate.

PRAYER: Dear God, give us the wisdom to use the disruptions in our schedules to your glory. For Jesus' sake. Amen.

Dorien K. Miles—Bremerton, Washington

Philippians 2:1–9   Name Writing

THOUGHT FOR TODAY: ". . . but rejoice that your names are written in heaven." Luke 10:20

When my oldest son first learned to write his name, he practiced it everywhere. He wrote it on his toys, on walls, and on posters in his room. Visitors remarked about seeing his name on the front door. Every time I opened a book, Bruce had left his mark. As much as we scolded, he simply could not confine his signature to paper. It seemed that no area of his life or ours was untouched by his name.

This is what Jesus wants us to do—leave no area of our lives untouched by his name. He wants to be on our innermost pages, as well as on the front door, where all can see him.

PRAYER: Lord, help me to let go of those areas of my life that I need to turn over to you. May your name be stamped on my life so clearly that others may see you through me. In Jesus' powerful name. Amen.

Freda Briggs—El Dorado, Kansas

Mark 4:24–34   Bubbles!

THOUGHT FOR TODAY: He will hold us in the hollow of his hand.

In his books Leo Buscaglia describes the invisible, protective bubble that we Americans are taught to use around ourselves as a defense against the invasion of our person by others. The bubble makes us prefer gifts rather than the tender, loving touch. The bubble keeps us defensive and selfish. It can also make us bitter and lonely.

Imagine Jesus with a bubble! We would know nothing about God's revelation of love. There would be no healing touch. Children would not know the care of a heavenly Father. It is obvious that if we desire to follow Jesus and serve God that our bubbles must burst. God is the disciple's sure defense; not an invisible bubble.

PRAYER: Lord God, help us to focus on serving others rather than defending ourselves from them. Amen.

John E. James—Glenville, West Virginia

Luke 22:14–20 — Time to Renew!

THOUGHT FOR TODAY: And he took bread . . . and gave unto them, saying . . . this do in remembrance of me. Luke 22:19 (King James Version)

From time to time I receive notices informing me that my subscription to a magazine or newspaper must be renewed. Unless I make the effort to renew, I will be cutting myself off from the news and fellowship of my Christian friends across the nation.

This is what happens at the Lord's table. It is a renewal experience. I have received inspiration for the challenges of life. I have given of myself to the challenges of community and world service. However, there comes the time when spiritual and physical energies run out like the subscription of a magazine. If I am wise, I will return to the source of spiritual renewal—the Communion table.

PRAYER: Hear me, O Lord. "Create in me a clean heart, O God, and renew a right spirit within me" (Psalm 51:10, King James Version). Amen.   *Richard L. James—Williamston, North Carolina*

John 14:4–6 — Finding the Way

THOUGHT FOR TODAY: Jesus said to him, "I am the way, and the truth, and the life; no one comes to the Father, but by me." John 14:6

The helicopter pilot had come from Cameroon to assist with the evangelism program for inaccessible Zairian villages. As the "whirlybird" swooped down into villages which could not be reached by conventional aircraft or by road, it was possible for the team members to bring the gospel to places which had never had a Christian ministry.

By making a circuit, it was possible for several teams to be working at once. Every third day, the pilot returned to take them to new stations. On this particular day, however, the pilot lost his way and could not find the village he sought. It was only when he retraced the exact route which he had previously taken and carefully watched his compass that he succeeded in finding his way. How often in life we miss our goal because we do not follow the way which is laid out for us in God's Word.

PRAYER: God, grant that we may reckon with the compass of your direction as we seek to follow the way of Christ. Amen.
Harriet B. Dowdy—Moanza, Zaire

Matthew 7:7–11   Meeting Our Needs

THOUGHT FOR TODAY: Every good thing bestowed and every perfect gift is from above, coming down from the Father of lights. . . . James 1:17 (New American Standard Bible)

You know how hard it is to keep a house neat so that you aren't embarrassed by unexpected company. With a little warning you can hide the clutter. Finally the house looks neat.

We all have spiritual closets where we hide what we don't want people to see. We hide things even from ourselves. But Paul says that we must make everything known to God—and in the process, to ourselves. "In everything let your requests [or desires] be made known to God" (Philippians 4:6, *New American Standard Bible*). Our desires shape our lives so we need to know what we really want.

There are two basic desires: First, each of us needs to know that we are of value. God assures us of that. Second, each of us needs to know that we are loved unconditionally. God can also fill this need!

PRAYER: God, we thank you for fulfilling our deepest needs when no one else can! In Jesus' name. Amen.   *Doris Davis—Decatur, Arkansas*

1 John 3:15   An Ugly Robin?

THOUGHT FOR TODAY: Be angry but do not sin; do not let the sun go down upon your wrath. Ephesians 4:26

One day I stood at my window watching a starling eat the scraps of bread I had thrown out for the birds. At one side stood a robin, fluffed and ugly, exuding hate from every feather tip. When he could contain his rage no longer, he made a flying tackle, giving the starling a vicious peck. Again and again he vented his wrath as anger mounted. His cheery "Chirr-up" became an angry squawk as he refused to "break bread with one so common."

I was amused until I remembered that people often act the same way. We who call ourselves Christians may say unkind words and carry chips on our shoulders. We often let petty dislikes become stumbling blocks of hate. How foolish we are to starve ourselves with spiritual crumbs when there is ample food at God's table and room for us all.

PRAYER: God, teach us that we may know your peace. In Jesus' name. Amen.   *Allene Boyd—Ash Grove, Missouri*

1 Peter 5:1–7   Does Jesus Care?

THOUGHT FOR TODAY: Cast all your anxieties on him, for he cares about you. 1 Peter 5:7

"Does Jesus Care?" by Lincoln Hall is an old, old hymn I've known all my life. Never have I heard it and been able to keep the tears back. When I played it as a child practicing the piano, the tears flowed so freely I could not see the notes.

"Does Jesus care when my heart is pained?" "Does he care when I've tried and failed?" "Does he care when I've said good-bye to the dearest on earth to me?" All the situations mentioned are worthy of tears, but now I know the real and important message of the song: Jesus *really cares.*

I lost my husband in a very tragic automobile accident, and I was severely injured. This old hymn has brought me much comfort: "O yes, he cares: His heart is touched with my grief." This message has dried my tears, and now I rejoice and praise him for his tender loving care.

PRAYER: O God, who delivers us from every evil and danger in life, help us to know and feel your loving care around us. In Jesus' name. Amen.   *Mossie E. Melson—Lafayette, Indiana*

Psalm 104:1–2, 5–6   Visualizing God's Power

THOUGHT FOR TODAY: He sends the springs into the valleys, which flow among the hills. Psalm 104:10 (New King James Version)

Last summer our family enjoyed long hikes in Rocky Mountain National Park in Colorado. One day at Ouzel Falls, we studied the enormous cascading water as it poured over huge boulders and fallen trees. While I absorbed this beautiful scene, I pondered it in a symbolic way.

The endless clear water represented God's love and power as it flowed through and around tree branches and boulders. To me those boulders represented the obstacles and problems we face. Yet the rushing water, like God's strong love, got around every boulder.

In the eyes of faith, may we see that God's loving purposes are more powerful than any obstacles or valleys of life. If we allow it to happen, God's love can make its way through any situation.

PRAYER: Creator God, help us to see your wondrous work in nature, and especially in lives yielded to you through Christ. Amen.

Charlotte Adelsperger—Prairie Village, Kansas

Matthew 6:7–15   "Just the Bus Driver"

THOUGHT FOR TODAY: Everyone is a person for whom Christ died.

We were a tour group on a bus to Eastern Canada and New England. It was a fall foliage trip combined with early American and Canadian history. The timing was right, the trees were beautiful, and the fellowship was good!

One of our number was the bus driver, Jim. But he was *more* than *just* the driver. He became a friend to everyone and soon called each of us by name. He went out of his way to be helpful.

Jim had been a music major in college, and one evening after a long day with still miles to go, he began to sing, charming us with his ability. The climax came on that last day when he sang as he drove us toward home.

This time the song was Mallotte's "The Lord's Prayer," and there was peace in our hearts.

PRAYER: Help us all, dear God, to use our talents for your glory. Amen.

Ralph E. Herrick—Topeka, Kansas

SEPTEMBER

--------------------------------- Day 1 ---------------------------------

Proverbs 22:1–9   A Good Name

THOUGHT FOR TODAY: A good name is to be chosen rather than great riches. . . . Proverbs 22:1

The maintenance man entered the hospital lounge where I was sitting with my husband, who was waiting to be called for lab work and x-rays. I noticed his calm, polite manner when he spoke courteously to a secretary and went about his work. The secretary called, "Mr. Garnett Poindexter."

Since my husband's illness, it is much easier for me to complete forms and supply needed information, so I went at once to the desk when his name was called. As I moved across the room I heard the worker ask my husband, "Are you Garnett Poindexter? I was named for a man named Garnett Poindexter. My father knew him," he said. "My father said he was a good man," he continued. "He was kind and caring. He was honest and fair to everyone. When I was born, my father named me after him because he liked and respected Mr. Poindexter so much."

PRAYER: Give us strength to live out the teachings of Christ, O Lord. Help us to choose our words wisely and act in a loving way. Amen.

Anne W. Poindexter—Richmond, Virginia

--------------------------------- Day 2 ---------------------------------

Mark 10:46–52   Waiting Room Realities

THOUGHT FOR TODAY: The power of almighty God is released only as we declare our personal faith and trust in God.

The television set in the waiting room was blaring as the characters played out their roles, but in the audience a very different kind of drama was being lived. Here was a faithful and close-knit family waiting for the final moment in a life; another family was spending their fifth week of waiting.

No one wrote his or her own script, but there was no question that each one received comfort and strength in these hours of testing as they gave themselves in faith to God. Each one was greatly empowered to face real-life drama as they believed in the Lord of real life.

PRAYER: Lord, to whom we can go, you alone have the words of everlasting life. Thank you for being there. In your name. Amen.

Lawrence L. Hoptry—Nitro, West Virginia

Numbers 6:22–27   Overcoming

THOUGHT FOR TODAY: "May the Lord bless you and protect you; may the Lord's face radiate with joy because of you. . . ." Numbers 6:24–25 *(The Living Bible)*

When Ralph Showers, a Baptist minister, lost both hands in an electrical accident, he became fitted with hooks. Calling himself the Happy Hooker, he entered the world of persons with disabilities and became more sensitive to the needs of those with deficiencies.

At Rainbow Acres, Arizona, he established a farm community of lifetime homes. These homes provide industry, fellowship, security, and a meaningful life for sixty adults who are mentally retarded.

With love, patience, and respect for the individual, Showers helps his residents develop skills, earn a modest income, and learn to make independent decisions.

Surely the Lord's face radiates with joy on Ralph Showers.

PRAYER: Our God, give me the courage to accept my deficiencies and find ways to bring you joy. In Jesus' name. Amen.

Mary A. Magers—Portland, Oregon

Ephesians 1:3–10   The Invasion

THOUGHT FOR TODAY: Yet to all who received him, to those who believed in his name, he gave the right to become children of God. John 1:12 (New International Version)

The space program is costly. Through our invasion of space, however, we have all been helped. New developments in medicine, science, agriculture, and clothing have come our way. We have learned new and exciting facts about the unknown universe. We have also increased our powers of communication.

God's invasion of earth was also costly. It cost the death of God's Son, Jesus Christ, on the cross. Through his death and resurrection, great benefits have come our way. We can become God's sons and daughters, have eternal life, and find peace and purpose for our lives. Our sins are forgiven. We also find out more about the love of God and can communicate with the One who made the universe.

PRAYER: Gracious God, we thank you for loving us so much that you took the first step to invite us into your family in Christ. Amen.

William K. Webb—Clifton, New Jersey

1 Thessalonians 4:11–12; Colossians 3:12–17; Ephesians 4:28

Motives for Work

THOUGHT FOR TODAY: Can anyone tell you are a Christian by the way you do your daily work?

Do you have a Christian philosophy of work? Do you have clearly defined motives as you go about your daily tasks, motives that are grounded in scriptural principles? Some are suggested in the passages cited above.

Through honest work the Christian seeks to support self and family and "not be dependent upon anybody" (1 Thessalonians 4:12, NIV). Through honest work the Christian is able to help those in need, as Paul admonishes in Ephesians 4:28. Sharing is a basic principle of the Christian life, leading us to work not merely to get but also to give.

Through honest work, however humble or significant, the Christian is able to exert a wholesome influence upon individuals and society (1 Thessalonians 4:12) and to glorify God (Colossians 3:17).

PRAYER: Help us, God, to show by the way we do our work that we are truly your children. In Jesus' name. Amen.

Oliver E. Peterson—Lansdale, Pennsylvania

Psalm 34:1–8

Seek God!

THOUGHT FOR TODAY: I sought the LORD, and he answered me, and delivered me from all my fears. Psalm 34:4

Standing alone in bitter cold on a street corner in a strange city waiting for a bus, I wondered anxiously how I would find my destination. Christian friends back home were praying for me, and that morning's Scripture had read, "I will never leave you nor forsake you."

How unprepared I was for God's exceeding riches! Also waiting for the bus was a young woman. Casual conversation revealed that she was employed in the very building for which I was searching, and she volunteered to show me the way. And God's blessings continued: God blessed me by placing helpful people where I needed them, by speaking through the Scriptures to my everyday fears, and by showing loving concern through persons in the church where I worshiped.

PRAYER: Dear God, enable us to place our anxieties and fears in your loving hands, knowing that you will never forsake us. Amen.

Ruth Fiscella—East Freetown, New York

Psalm 100 — Another Day

THOUGHT FOR TODAY: This is the day which the LORD hath made; we will rejoice and be glad in it. Psalm 118:24 (King James Version)

Can you imagine!" I exclaimed in amazement to my daughter one Sunday afternoon. "Tomorrow is another day!"

Cathy's mouth dropped open in astonishment; suddenly we burst into laughter. "I meant to say that tomorrow is another school day," I explained. The weekend had gone fast; *that* was the amazing fact.

Yet my words nagged at me all day. A warm sun made light and shadows on tall green grass; butterflies played around me. Birds chattered above me. What a feast for my eyes and ears! But tomorrow would be *another* day.

Since then, those words often ring in my ears as I wake up. The sun rises, the birds sing, I am alive! "Can you imagine, another day!" I exclaim to myself. "Another day to be a part of the miracle of life."

PRAYER: Dear God, teach us to see and hear, feel and love, and thus really live this day before us. In Jesus' name. Amen.

Dathene Stanley—Townshend, Vermont

133

John 6:5–14 — The Lad with a Lunch

THOUGHT FOR TODAY: Jesus can use whatever we give him willingly, as he used the lad's lunch, to work miracles.

The story of the feeding of the multitude is the only miracle related by all four of the Gospel writers. Only John speaks of the lad's contribution, however. According to Mark, Jesus asked the disciples to see how many loaves they had. John tells us that Andrew found the boy with five loaves and two fish, apparently the only food in the crowd. John says Jesus took the loaves and fish and gave thanks, then distributed them to the people. When the people had eaten all that they wanted, the disciples filled twelve baskets with the fragments left. How happy that lad must have been to know that Jesus had used what he had to perform such a miracle! His lunch had fed five thousand people.

PRAYER: Dear God, take whatever we have and multiply it as you see fit to feed those hungering for righteousness. Amen.

Ruth H. Short—Norman, Oklahoma

Psalm 95:1–7   Proper Worship

THOUGHT FOR TODAY: "For it's not *where* we worship that counts but *how* we worship. . . ." John 4:22 *(The Living Bible)*

Our church building is a masterpiece. Stained glass windows glow with sunlight and cast multicolored highlights on the altar. The soft blue decor speaks of peace.

As I worshiped in this atmosphere last Sunday morning, I noticed two women whispering throughout the introductory hymn. During the sermon, one man read the newspaper while another nodded to sleep.

Looking further, my eyes rested on a white head bent in prayer. A wall of serenity surrounded this woman. The thoughts in her mind softened her wrinkled face. As she raised her head, her smile of contentment shone brighter than the windows. The majority of the people in the sanctuary were in church; the woman was with God.

PRAYER: God, help me to remember that the value lies not in the beauty of the building but in the spirit of the worship.

Barbara Robidoux—Chicopee, Massachusetts

2 Timothy 2:14–16   Be Faithful, Be Consistent

THOUGHT FOR TODAY: Do your best to present yourself to God as one approved. . . . 2 Timothy 2:15

It is bad enough growing old naturally without having my children age me prematurely. Getting them off to school each day ages me. It takes three calls and one scream to get them out of bed. Then I referee the bickering over who uses the bathroom first. This is followed by "We never have anything good to eat for breakfast." By now time is running out. One screams that he'll be late for school, while the other is reading the comics. After driving them to school, I arrive back home exhausted, irritable, and out of sorts.

It is then that I remember that our natural desire is to avoid doing what we don't like to do. The task of learning to be a responsible person is very hard. Jesus showed us by how he lived and by what he did that life is lived responsibly to God and others.

PRAYER: I trust you, O God, in this day to help me do the things I may like to avoid doing. Make of me your servant. Amen.

Glenn C. Abbott—Sioux Falls, South Dakota

Mark 10:13–16   Unreserved Love

THOUGHT FOR TODAY: . . . And a little child shall lead them. Isaiah 11:6b

When baby Bryan was born with a harelip, Sarah refused to hold or feed him—until the doctor insisted. She couldn't stand to look at the gaping hole that extended into one nostril.

The doctor assured her that it could be corrected in a few months when he would start corrective surgery. In the meantime Sarah hid Bryan from prying eyes. The only people she couldn't hide him from were her husband and four-year-old Tommy. She had Tommy at her elbow when she fed and bathed Bryan.

The day came for Bryan's admission for surgery. As Sarah dressed him, Tommy asked, "Where are we taking Bryan, Mommy?"

"We're going to the hospital, and he's going to have his lip fixed so it will look like yours."

"But, Mommy, I love Bryan the way he is!"

PRAYER: O God, help us bury our pride and teach us to love as a small child—without reservations. Amen. *MaryLou Klingler—Phoenix Arizona*

135

John 9:1–12   Blind Faith

THOUGHT FOR TODAY: . . . God works for the good of those who love him . . . Romans 8:28 (New International Version)

A workman, out of work because his employer's business had failed, could see no hope for work in his recession-hit area. After prayer, with God's help he was led to take stock of his abilities and the needs around him and to start a successful repair and maintenance business that met a real community need.

If the man born blind had known that his affliction would demonstrate God's power for ages to come, he could have been thankful even for blindness. When we have faith to believe that out of every trouble God will give us a triumph, we, too, can praise God in adversity.

PRAYER: God, help me to love you and trust you in comfort and adversity so that I may honor you with my life. In Jesus' name. Amen.
Walter B. Wakeman—Calais, Maine

Psalm 19:1–6 Scene of Beauty

THOUGHT FOR TODAY: Draw nigh to God, and he will draw nigh to you. Cleanse your hands, ye sinners; and purify your hearts, ye double minded. James 4:8 (King James Version)

When viewing a scene of beauty while strolling a lonely country path, I experience contentment.

The scent of freshly cut hay fills my nostrils. As rabbits frolic in a field of wild flowers, the sun plays hide-and-seek amidst darkening clouds.

Suddenly the scene becomes gloomy. The wind increases, and trees bow under its strength. The clouds thicken; it's getting dark in the middle of the day. I am frightened by the threat of an inescapable storm.

As I tread onward, once again birds start singing. An array of blue, green, and yellow glistens off the rocks as the sun seeks to push through dense clouds.

Shadows cast their playful shapes and the quieted breeze enhances the finishing touches to this scene of beauty.

PRAYER: When the threat of a storm in nature or a storm in everyday life faces us, help us, God, to understand that your mighty hand is in complete control of all things. In Jesus' name. Amen.

136 *Rita J. Sullivan—Gardners, Pennsylvania*

Isaiah 30:15–19 In Quietness and Trust

THOUGHT FOR TODAY: In our fast-paced world, the Christian must learn that in quietness we learn to trust God.

There is a very important secret tucked away in the Bible. It is the secret of finding God's strength for each day. "In quietness and in trust shall be your strength" (Isaiah 30:15). Notice the two conditions: quietness and trust. How much time do you spend being quiet with God? The rush to the office, the habit of television, and endless errands take time that could be spent with God. Most of us go rushing through life, hectic and harried, pushed and pulled by hundreds of little issues that seek to rob us of our quiet time with God.

Today, will you trust God enough to spend ten, twenty, thirty minutes of quietness in God's presence? Isaiah reminds us that in so doing we will discover the very strength of God filling our lives.

PRAYER: Our Father, quiet our rushing minds. Help us to trust you enough to seek your presence so that we might experience your strength. Amen. *James H. McAllister—Millbrae, California*

Hebrews 13:2; James 2:1–4

Hospitality Without Partiality

THOUGHT FOR TODAY: The stranger we entertain today may be an "angel" who will bring blessings to us tomorrow.

Recently I toured the historic Sturgis Pretzel House in Lititz, Pennsylvania—the place where pretzels were first made in America. The tour guide told us that one day a hobo wandered into this bread bakery and begged for a piece of bread. The owner instead invited him to join him for dinner. In appreciation, the hobo gave the baker the recipe for *pretiolas* that he had brought over from his homeland. Soon pretzels were popular not only in Lititz but all over the country.

We never know the true worth of an individual based on his outward appearance. Nor do we know the blessing that an act of kindness will bring until *after* it is bestowed. That is why Jesus tells us to avoid being judgmental and to be kind to all those whose lives we touch.

PRAYER: Dear Lord, let me know to whom I can be especially hospitable today, either in word or in deed. In Jesus' name, I pray. Amen.

Sandi Cleary—Northfield, New Jersey

John 1:1–5

Light a Candle

THOUGHT FOR TODAY: The light from one small candle can bring a wanderer home.

It is better to light a candle than to curse the darkness." How often we have heard this quote, and what a good thing it is to do.

A few years ago my husband and I visited Cairo, Egypt. Of course, we visited the pyramids and even took a guided tour into the interior of one of them. The lighting was hardly adequate for finding one's way around. All at once the lights went out. Some members of the group became nearly panic-stricken.

My husband happened to have a very small flashlight in his pocket. Just that small beam of light did much to calm the tour members until the lights came on a little later.

Let us search for opportunities each day to "light a candle."

PRAYER: Dear Jesus, "take my hands and let them move at the impulse of your love," serving those to whom you lead me. Amen.

Erma Fajen MacFarlane—Columbia, Missouri

Psalm 23   Someone with a Purpose

THOUGHT FOR TODAY: ". . . how often would I have gathered your children together . . . and you would not." Matthew 23:37

In the days of the one-room school, seven-year-old Archie sat in the front row. When the older classes would go up front for geography lessons and would recite the countries and capitals of South America, Archie was intensely interested and followed each lesson. By the time the others had completed their study, the seven-year-old could repeat the countries and capitals of South America by heart. After he had become a pioneer missionary in Bolivia and had started what is today a thriving Christian mission, Archibald Reekie looked back to the experience in that one-room school and said, "Someone with a purpose was guiding my life."

PRAYER: Our God, help us to be receptive to your guiding hand in our lives. You alone know the way our feet should travel. Amen.

Duncan J. MacNab—Lafayette, Indiana

138

1 Kings 19:1–19   Overcoming Fear

THOUGHT FOR TODAY: Then he was afraid, and he arose and went for his life . . . . 1 Kings 19:3

Fear is all about: "What's that noise? Is someone in the house?" "Is that kid coming toward me going to grab my pocketbook?" "Is that lump in my breast malignant?" What does one do in the face of fear?

Elijah did three things. He ran. He became depressed. He slept. When Jezebel came after him, Elijah ran for three days into the wilderness.

Withdrawal is always a part of depression. Elijah sat under a broom tree and asked that he might die. He hurt so much that even death seemed better than what he was experiencing.

Then Elijah lay down and fell asleep. Some of us take to our beds when we are depressed. In his sleep Elijah heard God say, "Arise and get up! Get dressed! Get moving!"

You know the rest of the story. In a still, small voice God gave the answer to Elijah's fear.

PRAYER: Lord, let us remember that man who said, "We have nothing to fear but fear itself." Let us remember, even more, the Person who said, "Perfect love casts out fear." In Jesus' name we pray. Amen.

Richard L. Keach—Hartford, Connecticut

Isaiah 30:15–21   Those Who Wait

THOUGHT FOR TODAY: . . . blessed are all those who wait for him.
. . . Isaiah 30:18

In these busy times when nearly everyone is under pressure, waiting takes patience. To wait when the strong desire is to "get on with it" is frustrating. But to hurry, to speed things up, to compress life into days and weeks in order to get things done is contrary to the life pattern that God has created.

When we ask God for some needed blessing, we want an immediate answer. With God there is always a right time and place. God said, "In returning and rest you shall be saved; in quietness and in trust shall be your strength" (Isaiah 30:15). The quiet times give our souls time to catch up with our bodies. The right answer and direction will always come when we wait for it.

PRAYER: God, teach us how to pray and to have patience to wait for the answer. In Jesus' name. Amen.

Bennett F. Hall—Winchester, Kentucky

John 15:1–11   "Pruning" Time

THOUGHT FOR TODAY: ". . . for apart from me you can do nothing."
John 15:5

When I was a boy of six, my parents moved to a house with a large grape arbor. The vines then were reputed to be eighty years old. On a February day my father pruned them back so severely that I was alarmed. Yet the next summer found the vines beautifully covering the arbor and producing luscious grapes. Mother provided grape juice to our local church for Communion for fifty years.

I learned that long stems of the vine use up much nourishment from the root and do not leave enough food to produce healthy grapes. Pruning keeps the stems short and close to the vine.

Is not Jesus' instruction to "abide in him" pertinent? The closer we live to him, the more fruitful are our lives. A dynamic faith-relationship with him provides the divine guidance and inspiration necessary to produce deeds of worth and service.

PRAYER: Living God, prune bad habits, unworthy attitudes, and sinful activities from my life. Be the source of my strength. For Jesus' sake. Amen.

Raymond M. Veh—Thiensville, Wisconsin

Luke 5:12–16   Catch Me If You Can

THOUGHT FOR TODAY: But grow in spiritual strength and become better acquainted with our Lord and Savior Jesus Christ. 2 Peter 3:18 *(The Living Bible)*

Our cat, whom we definitely wanted to be a *house* cat, had gotten out again when the children, already late, went rushing off to school. It didn't matter that they didn't have time to play. The cat was off and running at her favorite game "Catch me if you can."

Do we sometimes play the same game with God? Do we say we want to know God better but then fail to give God more than just a few rushed minutes? Do we expect God somehow to catch us on the run?

The Scripture says that even long before daybreak Jesus went out alone to pray (Mark 1:35). The passage for today indicates that this was his common practice (Luke 5:16). Were we to follow his example, in what exciting ways might we also experience God's power in our lives?

PRAYER: God, forgive us for all those times when we are too busy for you. Help us to put you first. For Jesus' sake. Amen.

Marlene Bagnull—Drexel Hill, Pennsylvania

Luke 2:41–49   Don't Lose Him

THOUGHT FOR TODAY: Make sure Jesus is "in the company" each day.

Mary and Joseph had been about their religious duties. After Passover they started home with others who were also devout and intent upon the worship of God. Then, we are told, they, "supposing him to have been in the company, went a day's journey . . ." Luke 2:44 (KJV).

Last summer a cousin told me that the sermon that led her to become a Christian was preached on this Scripture. The minister ended by saying, "Take him now, lest you, too, lose him."

As church members we, too, get so absorbed in our church activities that we may take Jesus for granted. Surely since we are among Christians, he is there somewhere "in the company!" Let's be careful never to go a day's journey without being sure that *we* are at *his* side, lest, like Mary and Joseph, we lose him.

PRAYER: God, we know that we need you every hour. In Jesus' name. Amen.   *Lucena J. Kibbe—Utica, New York*

Colossians 1:9–10 No Small Deed

THOUGHT FOR TODAY: . . . to lead a life worthy of the Lord, fully pleasing to him, bearing fruit in every good work and increasing in the knowledge of God. Colossians 1:10

A young woman and her small son moved into my neighborhood. I went over and welcomed them. As we talked, I realized that she had been recently divorced and was very lonely. I told her about the neighborhood stores and churches. When I mentioned my faith in Christ, she immediately froze. After that, when I tried to be friendly, she avoided me.

One day I was baking a cake and felt the urge to bake one for my new neighbor, also. When I knocked at her door, I was afraid of how she would respond. I blurted out the words, "I felt God wanted me to make you this cake." She began to cry and said, "It's my birthday. How could you have known?"

PRAYER: Dear God, may I always be sensitive to the needs of others and respond in kind and loving ways for your sake. Amen.

Mary Huffman—Downingtown, Pennsylvania

John 1:6–14 What Are You Looking For?

THOUGHT FOR TODAY: Wisdom is before him that hath understanding; but the eyes of a fool are in the ends of the earth. Proverbs 17:24 (King James Version)

Easy answers! So much time is spent looking for easy answers!

Life is not composed of easy answers. It is like a man who wished for a bag of gold. A stranger appeared and said, "There is a bag of gold just waiting for you! Take this sack with you; someday you'll find it!" The man searched everywhere. Time went quickly. His sack became a stool, a pillow. He died. Those caring for "last things" discovered the sack. They found a seal which had not been broken in fifty years. Inside the sack were hundreds of gold coins. In a lifetime spent hunting for a treasure, he was a beggar sitting on a bag of gold.

We, too, fail to see the treasures around us in the everyday experiences placed there by God.

PRAYER: God, grant me the serenity to accept things I can't change, courage to change what I can, wisdom to know the difference. Amen.

Arthur H. Kuehn—Lewiston, Maine

..c 4:31–41   Casting Out Demons

THOUGHT FOR TODAY: And demons also came out of many. . . .
Luke 4:41

A woman who was emotionally disturbed came to Paul Tillich for help.
She was trying to explain her "demons" to him. Unperturbed, Tillich
said, "Every morning between seven and ten, I live with demons."

In his book, *Love and Will,* Rollo May says the demonic is both destructive and creative. When Paul Tillich looked at his demons for three
hours every morning and named them, he was released from their
destructive power, and he became creative.

One day Jesus was teaching in the synagogue. Suddenly, one of the
listeners began to shout. Jesus healed the man who was possessed by
a destructive demon. Luke says, "Jesus heals!" If anyone is in Christ,
that person is a new creation; the old destructive powers pass away.

PRAYER: Lord Jesus, let me give you the evil thoughts, attitudes, and
feelings that I have today. By your power I will be healed and whole.
Thanks be to God! Amen.   *Richard L. Keach—Hartford, Connecticut*

Isaiah 40:27–31   Expecting a Miracle

THOUGHT FOR TODAY: . . . he renews life within me. . . . Psalm 23:3
(New English Bible)

My muscles ached, my body was tired, and I felt more like crawling
back into bed than getting up. I remembered what someone had once
said, "Enthusiasm generates energy." But I thought of the day before
me: a dental appointment, a long meeting, a parade, chauffeuring children back and forth.

"Sorry, God," I said with regret, "no enthusiasm today."

Then I remembered those words from Isaiah: ". . . but they who wait
for the LORD shall renew their strength, they shall mount up with wings
like eagles . . ." (Isaiah 40:31). Suddenly, I wondered what kind of
miracle God could work in my hectic, demanding day. A quiet sense of
anticipation began to grow inside me.

PRAYER: My God, today let me let you give me the strength to mount
up with wings like an eagle. In Jesus' name. Amen.
                                          Dathene Stanley—Chiang Mai, Thailand

Psalm 18   Dependable

THOUGHT FOR TODAY: . . . I will liken him unto a wise man, which built his house upon a rock. . . . Matthew 7:24 (King James Version)

Matthew and the psalmist both speak of Jesus as a rock. This takes me back to my early girlhood days when I lived on a little rocky farm.

Daily I played with rocks. My playhouses were all made with them. I learned many things about rocks. I learned they remained where I left them; the wind never blew them away. They never wilted like the wild flowers that I picked. They never changed in either shape or color. They were always the same.

What better illustration of the Lord Jesus can we find today than the rock? Jesus is always there. He never deserts us. All we need to do is to reach out to him. I *know*, for I have felt his touch. Jesus certainly has been my solid Rock!

PRAYER: God, may I, too, be found dependable in your sight. In Jesus' name. Amen.   *Jessie Johnson Young—Mason City, Illinois*

1 John 4:7–16   Love in Action

THOUGHT FOR TODAY: Love of God and love of persons are closely entwined.

Love is to be translated into action. However, it is possible to be so active in good works that we miss the spirit of this genuine love.

If we were asked what we had done to show love for others, would we talk of our work on committees, of money given for missions, and of tray favors made for a nursing home? What *person* have we loved in Jesus' name?

We need group projects to accomplish work efficiently. Yet equally important is the work of one who takes a neighbor to the doctor or the retired couple who visit in a nursing home often.

Love is the personal touch. ". . . Love should not be just words and talk; it must be true love, which shows itself in action" (1 John 3:18, Good News Bible).

PRAYER: Loving God, we have experienced your love for us. Help us to love others. In Jesus' name. Amen.

Eleanor P. Anderson—Beckley, West Virginia

Isaiah 58:7–11   Passing By

THOUGHT FOR TODAY: When God's children are in need, you be the one to help them out. Romans 12:13 *(The Living Bible)*

A friend and I, with four children in tow, were making the rounds of the historic sights in Philadelphia. Excitedly the children pointed at the various buildings, quizzing us on our knowledge of colonial times. Spying a ledge around a modern bank, they scrambled up on it, laughing and chasing each other for half a block. Jumping down, they almost tripped over a derelict who was lying curled up on the pavement. Their exuberance changed to solemnity as the focus of their questions changed. "What's the matter with that man?"

As we walked around the man, I struggled to find answers for their questions as well as for the one that kept plaguing me deep within. Jesus would not have passed him by. Why did I?

PRAYER: Forgive us, God, for all the times we fail to risk involvement with human need. Help us to become more like your Son. Amen.

Marlene Bagnull—Drexel Hill, Pennsylvania

Psalm 51:1–17   The Old Made New

THOUGHT FOR TODAY: Purge me with hyssop, and I shall be clean; wash me, and I shall be whiter than snow. Psalm 51:7

The old dresser had been painted a drab green long before it was given to my in-laws. It had been blackened by smoke in a fire. When they bought a new bedroom set, they were going to discard it. Yet, the drawers were gently rounded; it had "claw feet" and dovetail construction. My husband felt sure it was a valuable antique—so he carted it home.

There it sat—hidden in a corner—grossly ugly!

Our son was in woodshop that year and needed a project; so we hauled the old dresser to school. We received progress reports, but when it came home, we didn't recognize it. It was a beautiful "bird's-eye" maple.

Our lives often appear scarred and useless, but Christ *sees* us and transforms us to what we were truly meant to be.

PRAYER: Thank you, Lord, for the transforming power of your love. Amen.

Lois E. Woods—Sumner, Washington

OCTOBER

─────────────────── Day 1 ───────────────────

Matthew 4:18–20   Wherever God Calls

THOUGHT FOR TODAY: The call of God can be to many fields of work and our task is to be ready whenever and wherever the call comes.

During our conversation in his office, he almost apologized for being there. It seems that when he was still a young man he heard the call to the ministry but he went instead into the field of education. He really had no need to feel remorse, for as I reflected upon his life, I knew that he had actually answered the call. His pulpit was a teacher's desk; his church house was a school building; his congregation was a group of youngsters.

The call of God to service does not always lead to the pulpit ministry. God has a place for each one of us to flourish. Our duty is to keep our spiritual eyes and ears open to God's call and then respond.

PRAYER: Remind me constantly, God, that Jesus served in little Judea, but he *did* serve! In Jesus' name. Amen.

Lawrence L. Hoptry—Nitro, West Virginia

146

─────────────────── Day 2 ───────────────────

Daniel 2:19–23   The Solution

THOUGHT FOR TODAY: There are answers when you use the right textbook.

Then God said, 'Let there be light'; and there was light" (Genesis 1:3, NKJV). That had always seemed no more than a simple statement. Light was the first step in forming our world. Today I read it again and there was light in my world—the light of understanding that God solves problems. Hadn't he made the world out of a dark formless mass?

Often when we are faced with a problem, we worry and fret. Our solution usually doesn't work because our minds, like the unformed world, are without God's touch. Then when we really seek God's assistance, there is a great change!

After we understand the real problem, the bright light of God's solution is revealed. It was always there; we just needed to remove the blindfold of self by seeking God's guidance.

PRAYER: Dear God, be patient with your children when they forget that any problem, big or small, can be brought to you. Amen.

Deloris Largent—Marion, Indiana

John 10:7–18   Abundant Life

THOUGHT FOR TODAY: "I came that they may have life, and have it abundantly." John 10:10

Jesus made this statement in telling a parable of the sheepfold. Sometimes when the sheep are in a fold, a thief comes to open the doors and steal them. Jesus said that he was not like that. He is a good shepherd. He came to bring abundant life.

Everyone has a different agenda for achieving abundant life. Here's a list from a Sunday church school class. Abundant life is:
• Digging in the dirt of my garden.
• Family and friends.
• Visiting the sick.
• Silence and meditation.

What is abundant life for you? A woman I know lived to be 101. I once asked her, "What is the secret of your long life?" She said, "Love for my family and my church." That was abundant life for her.

PRAYER: God, may good things happen for others today because they have met me. In Jesus' name. Amen.

Richard L. Keach—Hartford, Connecticut

Matthew 6:25–34   Tomorrow: In God's Hands

THOUGHT FOR TODAY: Fold the arms of your faith and wait in quietness until the light goes up in your darkness. George MacDonald

I am sorry we were not able to do as you had requested during surgery," the doctor said and went on to explain the reasons. After discussing the alternatives remaining, he went off on rounds.

The patient stared, almost unseeing, through the window that framed a sparkling fairyland of ice and snow, punctuated by a pair of cardinals at play. Disappointment was keen, even though she knew she was in no danger. Recovery would be slower; unanticipated limitations would have to be accepted—it *was* a bit of a "bummer." Watching the birds, she thought, *What if that careful surgeon had risked too much to try to give me what I wanted?* Would she be able to face tomorrow? Why not? The God of snow and birds and persons would be there!

PRAYER: God, our Creator and Sustainer, we thank you for your unstinting provision of *all* that we need each day. Amen.

Mildred Schell—Dayton, Ohio

Psalm 107:1–9   A Thankful Heart

THOUGHT FOR TODAY: A thankful heart is an offering of love to God.

Recently released from the hospital, my eighty-year-old mother was enjoying the visit of friends. As we read Psalm 23 together, her face was a picture of contentment. Holding onto her chair for support, she rose shakily to bid good-bye to her guests. Her bright blue eyes sparkled as she paraphrased the sixth verse, applying the Psalm to her own experience, "Surely goodness and mercy *have* been with me all the days of my life." She said it with conviction. She had trod gallantly through the depression years, heartache, disappointment, and declining health, but thanksgiving was her way of life. She refused to allow discontent and peevish pouting to mar her walk with Jesus Christ.

PRAYER: Dear God, may a spirit of thanksgiving permeate my life and be an expression of love and trust in you. Amen.

Florence E. Parkes—Oxon Hill, Maryland

John 20:24–28   Our Lord and Our God

THOUGHT FOR TODAY: When we see Christ as *our* Lord and *our* God, he becomes a very real person for us.

My wife and I studied under William Barclay some years ago at the University of Saint Andrew in Scotland. He made it perfectly clear to us that Jesus is more than a memory to be called to mind; he is a person to be met and experienced. Barclay added that the sacrament of the Lord's Supper is certainly a confrontation with the risen Lord.

We encounter the Savior whether it be at the moment of conversion, when we find him helping us make decisions, or at a time when we renew our commitment to him at the Communion table. It is at these times that we become vividly aware of Christ as the person who leads us beside still waters and into green pastures of love and grace.

Truly, we must see him as *our* Lord and *our* God!

PRAYER: God, forgive us for those times when we have not looked beyond ourselves to the person of Jesus Christ. Amen.

Paul Foster McKinley—Chariton, Iowa

Philippians 4:4–9   Think Jesus

THOUGHT FOR TODAY: . . . to be spiritually minded is life and peace. Romans 8:6 (King James Version)

The apostle Paul often directs us to keep good things in the mind. In Philippians 4:8–9, he advises us to think on things the way he practiced them. He directs us to think on things that are true, honest, just, pure, lovely, and of good report.

Solomon said, "As he thinketh in his heart, so is he . . ." (Proverb 23:7, KJV). The ultimate is to be spiritually minded, which results in life and peace. There is no better way to reach this than to *think* Jesus.

• To think Jesus is to enjoy his friendship.
• To think Jesus is to enjoy his companionship.
• To think Jesus is to flood our living with joy.

PRAYER: God, let the same mind be in me which was in Christ Jesus as he lived and as he died. Amen.   *Henry Toews—Porterville, California*

Psalm 19:1–8   Give of Yourself

THOUGHT FOR TODAY: The testimony of the Lord is sure, making wise the simple. Psalm 19:7 (King James Version)

Please talk to me, I'm lonely." This was the inscription on the badge worn by one young man standing on a milk crate at Speaker's Corner in Hyde Park in London, England.

Through conversation my husband and I determined that this young man did not want friends; he just wanted to talk. "I never smile," he said, "because a smile is the beginning of friendship. A smile leads to an exchange of names and this requires that I give something of myself away and I'm not willing to do that."

Many people we meet each day do not express their feelings as openly as did this young man, yet there are many lonely people among our daily contacts. Why not share a smile and conversation with them and give something of yourself away?

PRAYER: "Let the words of my mouth and the meditation of my heart be acceptable in thy sight, O Lord, my strength and my redeemer." Amen.   *Marilyn D. Harris—Hatboro, Pennsylvania*

Genesis 1:1–13 God's Wonderful Creation

THOUGHT FOR TODAY: And God saw that it was good. Genesis 1:12

My hometown is in a valley where two rivers converge and form the Kansas River. The soil in the riverbed is rich, and most years the area along the river is green and beautiful with many trees. When one takes the road from the city south to Interstate 70 a change takes place. The highway climbs up out of the lowlands to a region of short grass and sweeping vistas. Here and there herds of cattle can be seen. I never fail to be thrilled by the vastness of the high prairie and sky. Two verses come without bidding into my mind—"I lift up my eyes to the hills. From whence does my help come? My help comes from the LORD, who made heaven and earth" (Psalm 121:1–2).

I am constantly awed by the greatness of God's creation. As far as I can see and beyond that, God created it all. God is still making and remaking it with wind and rain, heat and cold.

PRAYER: Oh, God, how magnificent are all your works and wonderful beyond our imagination. Thank you, God. Amen.

Martha VanDam Kingsley—Green Lake, Wisconsin

1 Corinthians 9:19–27 Parts of a Whole

THOUGHT FOR TODAY: I become all things to all men, that I may save some. . . . 1 Corinthians 9:22 *(Good News Bible)*

The sign above the basin read, "Pick the stone that best represents you." I studied the stones. Was I the smooth, flat one? The shiny black one? The perfectly round red one? My fingers touched a rough, gray rock, mottled with a spiderweb of quartz. I lifted it, brushed away the wetness, then closed my palm over it. I sat in church, caressed its roughness, and wondered why I had chosen it.

I realized that my life is like that rock. My life's outward appearance is solid, all together. Yet as I examine my life more closely I find that it, too, is fragmented, split asunder by the demands of being a wife, mother, and wage-earner. It is held together in its fragmentation by the only cohesive agent that works: God's love.

PRAYER: Thank you, Lord, for love so great, so uniting, that we can be all you want us to be and yet be one. Amen.

Lois E. Woods—Sumner, Washington

Psalm 33:18–22   Leaning on God

THOUGHT FOR TODAY: Leave your troubles with the LORD.... Psalm 55:22 *(Good News Bible)*

As I write this, hurricane "Alicia" is barrelling along toward Texas, and I am remembering thirty years ago when "Barbara" swished up the North Carolina coast.

My family and I live on Harkers Island, which is ten feet above sea level. During the first hurricane our house shook and groaned as the winds and waves increased. The eerie silence of the "eye" lasted forty-five minutes and then the one-hundred-ten-mile-an-hour winds howled again. Exhausted from hours of tension and stress, we decided to turn our anxieties over to God, and fully clothed, we lay down to rest. Worry was lifted from our minds; peace entered our hearts; and we awakened four hours later to find "Barbara" merely a gentle rain!

PRAYER: God, help us to remember that you are willing to carry all our worries and problems. Hold our hands as we lean on you. Amen.

Jean M. Hurt—Jacksonville, Florida

Matthew 11:25–30   Healing in a Broken World

THOUGHT FOR TODAY: "O man of little faith, why did you doubt?" Matthew 14:31b

There's a saying, "Be very patient with everyone you meet, for he or she is struggling with some kind of problem." A friend, co-worker, or family member becomes extra irritable or edgy or uptight, and we begin to suspect that some personal problem is devouring his or her insides. A wise observer of human beings once said, "When someone rants and raves about the world condition, he or she isn't telling you anything about the world but is trying to tell you something about the condition of his or her heart, mind, and soul."

Stress, strain, tension, pressure, and problems keep knocking on our doors every day. At such times we can lean on the church. We can gain strength from friends of like faith. In this spiritual environment, burdens are lifted and broken lives are put back together.

PRAYER: O God, you understand the pressures we feel. Grant us the insight and courage to let others help us as you also help us. Amen.

Gary L. Reif—West Lafayette, Indiana

————————————— Day 13 —————————————

John 11:31–46   Burden-Bearers

THOUGHT FOR TODAY: We who are strong in the faith ought to help the weak to carry their burdens. . . . Romans 15:1 *(Good News Bible)*

Someone I know had lost his best friend in a freak accident. He was overwhelmed with grief and sorrow at the sudden loss of his companion. At the funeral, while the sorrow-struck friend wept uncontrollably, an acquaintance approached him and remarked, "Why are you so broken up? You should envy him because he's with the Lord now."

Sometimes we mistakenly judge a reaction to grief or pain as weakness. We confuse true faith with stoic acceptance. When Jesus faced the death of his friend Lazarus, he did not rebuke those around him who were letting their grief show. On the contrary, he shared in their grief. Through God's grace we can also be burden-bearers like our Lord.

PRAYER: God, please help me not to run from the burdens of others, but to help carry them. In Jesus' name. Amen.

Max Wardlow—Fillmore, Missouri

————————————— Day 14 —————————————

Isaiah 49:6; John 3:16–17;   The World in Thai
Matthew 28:19–20

THOUGHT FOR TODAY: I will make you a light to the nations. . . . Isaiah 49:6 *(New English Bible)*

Out of the corner of my eye I saw the display of globes in the Chiang Mai bookstore. But Cathy stopped before it and called to me, "Look, Mom! Here's our world; it's in Thai!"

I smiled. Our world isn't in Thai; it's in English. No, it isn't, I realized. She's right and I'm wrong. Here's our world and it's in Thai and Chinese and Russian and Kikongo and in languages of which I've never heard. It's a world of Buddhists and Hindus and agnostics as well as Christians.

It is this world that God loved so much that he sent his Son—this world of strange people, strange languages, strange likes and dislikes. It is this world that God calls me to learn to know and to love. My comfortable community must give way to a sometimes uncomfortable, unfamiliar world—the world that he who sends me loves so much.

PRAYER: Dear God, help me enlarge my world to include all those made in your image and loved by you. In Jesus' name. Amen.

Dathene Stanley—Townshend, Vermont

─────────────────────── Day 15 ───────────────────────

1 Corinthians 1:21–31   Eccentrics

THOUGHT FOR TODAY: Ye are . . . a peculiar people. 1 Peter 2:9 (King James Version)

Conformity is the way of life for almost everyone. The only time we are comfortable being different from the rest of the world is when we can be different in a group. We thus gain from each other and hide a little within the crowd.

In terms of motion and balance an eccentric is something that is off-center, and thus turns erratically and unevenly. A camshaft, which is a vital part of an automobile engine, is an eccentric. As an engine needs a camshaft, so the world needs the Christian to give it direction and moral value. Yet in the eyes of the world, a Christian is an eccentric.

As those who are different, we need the church, our group where we can find support and encouragement. We may be "eccentric" for Christ, but it helps greatly that we don't have to stand out all alone.

PRAYER: Thank you, God, for those who stand with me in the faith. Help me conform to your will today. In Jesus' name. Amen.

Walter B. Wakeman—Rockland, Maine

153

─────────────────────── Day 16 ───────────────────────

Matthew 9:1–13   The Ugliest Word

THOUGHT FOR TODAY: Then Peter opened his mouth and said, Of a truth I perceive that God is no respecter of persons. Acts 10:34 (King James Version)

Back in the 1950s I was privileged to see Edward R. Murrow's television interview with Carl Sandburg. I remember one thing from that interview to this day. "What is the ugliest word in the English language?" Mr. Murrow asked. Without hesitation Carl Sandburg replied, "Exclusive. It shuts out too many people."

Yet many people pride themselves in belonging to exclusive clubs, living in exclusive neighborhoods.

In his day Jesus was accused of not being exclusive enough because he ate with publicans and sinners. His response silenced his critics. "I am not come to call the righteous, but sinners to repentance" (Matthew 9:13b, King James Version).

PRAYER: Dear God, let us not be concerned with how others see us but with how you see us. Amen.

Bessie Bortner Scherer—Glen Rock, Pennsylvania

John 1:4–5; Matthew 5:14–16   The Light Within

THOUGHT FOR TODAY: We are the light through whom God's light shines.

I had seen the framed stained-glass dove in the bookstore. It was beautiful. "How I'd like to have that," I thought. For several months I watched and waited, hoping that it would go on sale.

Then one morning I decided that on sale or not, I would have it. I hung it joyfully in the window near my desk. It was beautiful. Surely, this would be a testimony for passersby. I went outside and to my disappointment only the frame and a dull blur could be seen. That night with lights on the inside, I went out to look. Oh, yes, the dove was visible. Then I remembered, it's the light within that reveals.

All the Christian symbols and trappings I might own or wear are meaningless unless Christ, the light of the world, is within.

PRAYER: O great Creator, we praise you for the light which you sent to us. Enable us to be light to one another, truly illuminating this dark world. In the name of Christ. Amen.

Grace T. Lawrence—Mechanicsburg, Pennsylvania

154

John 16:5–15   The Bank of the Holy Spirit

THOUGHT FOR TODAY: I can find the depth of God's riches inside me by using them for God's glory today.

The bank at the Leonardo da Vinci Airport in Rome is called BANCO DI SANTO SPIRITO, the Bank of the Holy Spirit. What a great name for God's people. We are the bank of the Holy Spirit. Once we have accepted Christ as our Lord and Savior, God gives us his Holy Spirit to live within us. He deposits God's love, joy, peace, patience, kindness, goodness, faithfulness, gentleness, and self-control in our lives. He makes the deposits. We make the withdrawals.

When we take God's love and use it to love the unlovely, he deposits more love. When we claim God's peace and use it to still our anxious hearts and the hearts of others, he gives us more peace. The more we use, the more God gives. We only need to be more aware of God's deposits and use them all to his glory.

PRAYER: Gracious God, may we use your qualities today to help draw the world closer to you, for Jesus' sake. Amen.

William K. Webb—Clifton, New Jersey

Psalm 98:1–6   Praise God

THOUGHT FOR TODAY: There are many ways in which we can praise our Maker.

Music has long been used in praising God. There are many passages in the Bible in which musical instruments are mentioned. In our modern day there are many musical instruments, and more than a few are used in praising God.

There are other forms of music, too. How about the lovely birdsong often heard at eventide? Surely we can think only good thoughts and join in praising God while listening to this beautiful music.

There is also the music of happy, laughing children. Who can deny that perhaps God considers their singing and joyful laughter some of the most acceptable music of all!

Whether by instrument, singing birds, or laughing and singing children, all join in praising God!

PRAYER: Help us, God, to encourage all people to join us in praising you. In Jesus' name. Amen.   *Erma Fajen MacFarlane—Columbia, Missouri*

Colossians 2:6–12   Rooted in Him

THOUGHT FOR TODAY: . . . continue to live in him, rooted and built up in him. . . . Colossians 2:6 (New International Version)

I have been told that among the thousands of islands scattered over the southwestern part of the Pacific Ocean is one island so situated that no wind can hit it. The trees growing on that island are so weak that they can be pushed over by a human.

Trees growing on neighboring islands, where winds blow frequently and tropical storms periodically hit, are able to withstand strong winds. No person could possibly push over a single tree. Those trees have been strengthened by what might seem like enemy forces.

We are like trees. If we lived our lives with nothing occasionally coming against us, we would be too weak to stand the hurricane forces that attack us. The winds that blow upon us cause us to push our spiritual roots deep into the soil of God.

PRAYER: God, cause our roots to grow deep into you so that we may grow strong and vigorous. Amen.

Marie Shropshire—Wichita Falls, Texas

Numbers 13:25–33　　　How's Your Point of View?

THOUGHT FOR TODAY: Forward or backward—where do you go from here?

In this reading from the Book of Numbers we find the Israelites displaying a fear of the future and a lack of faith. It is a timeless issue. This has been a problem of the church in all ages, in all times, in all generations. This incident should serve to constantly remind us that when all else is cleared away, it is faith in God that leads the way.

Our cue comes from Caleb: continue in our faith and belief in God, don't be anxious, keep hope, hold to a vision, display a willingness, and be ready to sacrifice. It is the point of view that makes the difference. What about your view of life? Caleb's point of view can be ours! Let's claim it!

PRAYER: Speak to us, Lord, help us to hear what you have to say. Help us to act on what you show to us. Amen.

Arthur H. Kuehn—Lewiston, Maine

Luke 22:7–20; Acts 1:8　　　The Tie that Binds

THOUGHT FOR TODAY: To come to the Lord's Table is to enjoy one of the highest privileges afforded the Christian.

It must have been a solemn occasion for the disciples as they ate the Passover supper with Jesus and sadly began to realize that this might indeed be the last meal they would share with the Lord they had come to know so intimately. One wonders what their thoughts and conversation might have been could they have known how many countless times the happenings of that night would be repeated in the centuries to come. How great their amazement could they have looked into the future to this very day when hundreds of millions of believers throughout the world would meditate upon the words first spoken in their hearing.

We who share in the observance today have the benefit of knowing the whole story that was only beginning to unfold for those disciples in the upper room. Their faithful witness in obedience to the Lord's commission, and the witness of those who have come after, has brought to the Lord's Table this day peoples of every race and color, every tongue and nation, to proclaim that Jesus Christ is Lord.

PRAYER: Thank you, God, for all those who meet with us today at the Table of our Lord as members of the family of God. Amen.

Oliver E. Peterson—Lansdale, Pennsylvania

Ephesians 6:4   Rooted in Christ

THOUGHT FOR TODAY: Train up a child in the way he should go, Even when he is old he will not depart from it. Proverbs 22:6 (New American Standard Bible)

Daily I pass by a newly planted tree struggling to grow. It has been sadly neglected and left to grow on its own. As a result, the trunk is growing horizontal instead of stretching upward toward the heavens. Evidently the owner wasn't concerned enough about the little tree to provide a strong support to assure that it would grow tall and straight.

Unfortunately many parents are as neglectful of their children's spiritual growth. They provide for the child's physical being, even to the point of overindulgence. The latest styles in clothing are provided and the choicest schools are chosen, but the feeding of the child's soul receives little or no thought. Instead of growing heavenward, the child's growth is in the wrong direction. As the little tree needed strong support, children need even more support of loving Christian parents.

PRAYER: God, please help parents to lovingly discipline their children so that they may grow to be your children also. Amen.

Norma C. Sanders—Sandborn, Indiana

157

Matthew 20:1–16   God's Generosity

THOUGHT FOR TODAY: . . . for God loves a cheerful giver. 2 Corinthians 9:7

A woman client of the famous attorney Clarence Darrow felt grateful to Darrow for his efforts on her behalf. At the close of the case, she hurried up to him and said, "Oh, Mr. Darrow, I don't know how I can ever thank you for what you have done for me!" Darrow courteously nodded; then he replied, "Madame, ever since the Phoenicians invented money, there has been a wonderful way to express your thanks!"

The same words might be applied whenever we feel thankful for God's generosity toward us. A wonderful way to express our gratitude is through our generous giving of our money to share in God's ministry.

There is a bumper sticker: Please Be Patient: God Isn't Finished with Me Yet. In God's generosity, God never is finished with us!

PRAYER: Our God, make us grateful for your generous ways and aid us in becoming more like your Son, in whose name we pray. Amen.

Darrell Heidner—Wichita, Kansas

Psalm 96:1–6, 10–13   Do Tell!

THOUGHT FOR TODAY: You are my witnesses in the home, in the town, in the country, and even to foreign countries.

A woebegone eleven-year-old boy came out of Pillsbury Hall at Green Lake, Wisconsin, as I approached. He said, "The dining room isn't open."

I explained that if the Lake View dining room wasn't open, the Veranda Room would be used for meals. After breakfast I found him waiting for me outside. He said, "If you hadn't told me, I wouldn't have had any breakfast. Thank you."

Many years ago in South China a military man gave his testimony of his joy in the Lord, but he added, "I was in a Christian home in west China during the war. Why didn't the people in the home tell me about Christ? I could have missed knowing about the way of salvation!"

Some may miss because we fail to tell. Surely we miss the joy of sharing if we don't tell.

PRAYER: Help us, God, always to tell of your blessings, our joys, and our knowledge of our Savior, Jesus Christ. In his name we pray. Amen.

Louise M. Giffin—Claremont, California

158

Psalm 118:23–29   Days of Our Life

THOUGHT FOR TODAY: So teach us to number our days, that we may apply our hearts unto wisdom. Psalm 90:12 (King James Version)

On my sixty-fourth birthday I received a card from my niece with a picture of her new son enclosed. On the back she wrote his name and age: Adam, three days old.

As I looked at the little child of three days, I thought of the days of life, the joys, challenges, friendships, jobs, memories, and the greatest of blessings—God's own loving care that fills our days. Life is made up of days and is a magnificent gift beyond our understanding.

I was amazed when I discovered that I have been given over 23,376 days that have been filled with God-given blessings. Should we not stop and thank our God for this day of life? "This is the day which the LORD hath made; we will rejoice and be glad in it" (Psalm 118:24, KJV).

PRAYER: We thank you, dear God, for the days of our lives and for the many blessings that you give us each day. Amen.

Myrtle Nelson—Quincy, Illinois

1 Corinthians 12:1–11   Enjoying Gifts

THOUGHT FOR TODAY: The Spirit's presence is shown in some way in each person, for the good of all. 1 Corinthians 12:7 *(Good News Bible)*

There are some gifts that are private, meant to be enjoyed by oneself. Other gifts may be enjoyed by many, like the gift of a beautiful voice or the talent to entertain in a gracious way. Who has not enjoyed seeing someone getting the gift of a box of candy and then sharing it with whoever is present?

One of the joys of belonging to a church is the opportunity of sharing in the experiences of others. Even sharing sorrows brings a certain amount of deep satisfaction as we give the gift of love and support to others. Jesus said we are not to hide our light under a bushel. Surely this means also that that which lights up our lives is to be shared.

Envy begrudges another person something valued or something enjoyed. The Christian message is that we are not only to enjoy the gifts of others but also, in Christ, to benefit from them as well.

PRAYER: Thank you, God, that I do not have to have every talent myself but can enjoy the gifts of others. Amen.

Frank Koshak—Prairie Village, Kansas

Psalm 90:10–17   Shared Beauty

THOUGHT FOR TODAY: And let the beauty of the LORD our God be upon us. . . . Psalm 90:17 (King James Version)

Sometime ago in Brattleboro, Vermont, a building on Main Street burned, leaving an ugly, gaping cellar hole.

One day, as I was hurrying down Main Street hill, I almost collided with an elderly woman. As I sidestepped, she touched me and said, "Oh, isn't that beautiful!"

I was startled. I could see no beauty. Then I noticed that she was pointing toward the cellar hole. There by the crumbling, blackened wall was a small sumac, clad in autumn's brilliant red.

As we stood there sharing this lovely sight, I was very thankful for this thoughtful person who had stopped my racing footsteps so that I might share with her a bit of God's beauty.

PRAYER: Dear God, help us to pause, to see, and to share with others your beautiful world. In Jesus' name. Amen.

Bea Pierce—Townshend, Vermont

Psalm 103:8–14   God Sees the Heart

THOUGHT FOR TODAY: ". . . man looks on the outward appearance, but the LORD looks on the heart." 1 Samuel 16:7

Our family was walking from the motel where we were staying to a nearby coffee shop. As we strolled, I could see ahead of us at the edge of the sidewalk a rather scraggly looking bush—ugly, really. As we approached it, I could see tiny yellow blooms on it. Then we stood beside it. I stooped down to examine it more closely, and I could see at the center of these delicate little yellow blossoms, a dark velvety rust color. The blossoms were enchantingly beautiful.

Ah, just so it is with us! Our God looks not on our outward appearance but at our hearts. Often God sees there the beauty that others may not see.

PRAYER: Dear God, thank you for seeing the beauty that is in us. May we in turn see the beauty in others. Amen.

J. Jewel Tilden—Claremont, California

Matthew 6:25–34   First—God's Kingdom

THOUGHT FOR TODAY: "But seek first his kingdom and his righteousness, and all these things shall be yours as well." Matthew 6:33

I was working long hours, approaching job burnout, and spending very little time with my family. One evening when I came home for a quick dinner before returning to work, my little boy said, "Dad, are you going to another meeting tonight? When are you ever going to have time for me?"

His question stopped me cold. I knew what he said was true. I wasn't home very much and hardly knew my kids. The money I was making was not bringing me nor my family the good life. At year's end I found another job, and my family and I now have time for one another.

How quickly, how easily, we lose sight of what's really important in life! It is simply keeping our priorities straight—" . . . seek first his kingdom and his righteousness, and all these things shall be yours as well."

PRAYER: Dear God, may we slow down our lives, spend more time with our families, and be grateful for the spiritual blessings of life. In Jesus' name. Amen.   *Ivan Knapp—St. Marys, Ohio*

Ephesians 3:16–19   A Step-By-Step Guide to Life

THOUGHT FOR TODAY: . . . but these are written that you may believe that Jesus is the Christ, the Son of God. . . . John 20:31

I've just begun to read a book, *Perspective Made Easy,* and I hope the author means just that. He calls it a step-by-step method for learning the basis of drawing.

Day by day I am more firmly convinced that the true perspective of all Christian living is found, step-by-step, in God's Word. This Author *means* what is written. The purposes of the Word of God are to lead us to Christ and to make our Christian pathway clear.

Every phase of Christian living grows out of the study of God's Word. If we neglect it, our lives grow more and more prayerless; our love and our service, lukewarm at best. But the more we read the Word of God, the more we will pray, the more we will love, the more we will desire God's will for our lives.

PRAYER: God, help us day by day to walk in the light of your Word. In Jesus' name. Amen. *Helen Fricke—Greenville, South Carolina*

NOVEMBER

John 10:11–18   Knowing One Another

THOUGHT FOR TODAY: ". . . that all of them may be one, Father, just as you are in me and I in you." John 17:21 (New International Version)

A family went to the movies one evening, and on the way in the young man of the family stopped by the refreshment stand to buy some popcorn. By the time he entered the theater the lights had been dimmed. He walked up and down the aisles, but evidently didn't see his family. Finally he shouted out, "Does anyone know me?"

Sometimes people shout that in our churches. Newcomers shout that because they need the friendship a church can offer. At other times we hear the cry of a long-term member who never felt welcome. At times we find just how much it means to be known by our church family. Remembering how much that means to us, let's share that with others.

PRAYER: Dear God, may we share your gift of love with others. Let there be no strangers in our midst. In Jesus' name. Amen.

Stephen K. Fisher—Marshfield, Missouri

Matthew 7:7–11   No Matter Too Small

THOUGHT FOR TODAY: He who did not spare his own Son . . . how will he not also, along with him, graciously give us all things? Romans 8:32 (New International Version)

A bakery truck drove up to a home in which I was visiting. Some weeks before, a teenage son living there had bought a box of doughnuts. The box read, "one dozen," but there were only eleven doughnuts in the box. The boy wrote to the company. The company sent a driver there with a whole new box. As the driver was leaving, he said, "There is no matter too small for us to investigate."

When the Bible tells us to cast all our cares on God because he cares for us, it is telling us that there is no matter too small for God to be concerned about. Whatever your concerns are today, take them to him.

PRAYER: God, we bring our concerns, both large and small, before you today in complete confidence, through Christ our Lord. Amen.

William K. Webb—Clifton, New Jersey

Psalm 119:129–136 God's Flashlight

THOUGHT FOR TODAY: The entrance of thy words giveth light. . . . Psalm 119:130 (King James Version)

My flashlight's beam punctured the blackness as I trudged up the forest path to our vacation cabin. Its tiny circle of light helped me to avoid the ruts and protruding rocks that made the trek hazardous.

As I proceeded slowly, I thought how life is like an unfamiliar pathway. My life trail winds into unknown blackness that my flashlight can't penetrate. I can't see the obstacles and pitfalls I'll encounter in the future. However, I'm not without direction for my life journey. God's Word, the Bible, sheds light on my path.

PRAYER: Dear Lord, thank you for your Word and the light it brings into my dark world. Amen. *Nancy Witmer—Manheim, Pennsylvania*

John 14:1–3; Jude, vv. 24–25 Homecoming

THOUGHT FOR TODAY: And he is able . . . to bring you . . . into his glorious presence with mighty shouts of everlasting joy. Jude, v. 25 *(The Living Bible)*

The first year I worked some distance from home, a co-worker and I accepted a ride in the open trunk of a friend's car in order to get home for a holiday. Even today, this intense desire to be home for certain special days causes many to brave all obstacles.

This craving to see loved faces, to feel a welcoming embrace, and to breathe in the unmistakable smells of home is not confined to holidays alone. All who have left a loving home for an extended period of time know it.

As exciting and as memorable as these homecomings are, Jesus and Jude tell us that the greatest homecoming of all is yet to come. One can imagine entering that awesome, glorious land feeling very small and unworthy. What an overwhelming thought to consider being welcomed with mighty shouts of everlasting joy!

PRAYER: Our God, we thank you for the love of family and friends. With grateful hearts we accept your divine grace that makes a heavenly homecoming possible. Amen. *Mary A. Magers—Portland, Oregon*

Ephesians 4:23–32   Asking Forgiveness

THOUGHT FOR TODAY: Be kind to one another, tenderhearted, forgiving one another, as God in Christ forgave you. Ephesians 4:32

A popular movie of not long ago brainwashed people into believing that "love means you never have to say you're sorry." Yet just the opposite is true. An unselfish love means being willing to admit you're wrong.

Sometimes I find this hard to do. So I try to be resourceful in telling my loved ones I'm sorry. Perhaps I bake my husband an un-birthday cake. When he smacks his lips appreciatively, the ice is broken and I can communicate my apologies. I may stick a note in my son's lunch, or on his pillow—sometimes in corny poetry.

Of course, there's nothing that surpasses a face-to-face, straight-from-the-heart encounter, with those healing words, "I'm sorry. Please forgive me."

PRAYER: Lord, when I ask your forgiveness first, it's easier to ask it of others. May I not postpone this act of love. Amen.

Shirley Pope Waite—Walla Walla, Washington

1 Corinthians 15:20–26   We Shall Live Again

THOUGHT FOR TODAY: God does not want Christians to sorrow after the loss of their loved one in Christ, as those who have no hope.

At last I had what must be one of God's most delicate and beautiful creations: a bleeding heart. It is a perennial plant with a curved stem holding small, pink, heart-shaped blossoms like tiny balloons. A droplet of "blood" is suspended from each. The plant was a source of real joy that spring. About mid-summer, however, the plant turned brown and died for no apparent reason. I couldn't understand it. The plants around it were thriving, and I had loved it so much.

The next spring, as I was working in my flower bed, I couldn't believe my eyes. My bleeding heart was coming up again!

I then learned that this was the natural pattern for this plant. This reminded me of the resurrection. Our loved ones in Christ are taken. We don't understand why, but we know they shall live again.

PRAYER: Dear Lord, thank you for the hope that we shall again see our loved ones in Christ. Amen.   *Opal Stoner—Hutchinson, Kansas*

Psalm 104:10–24   The Good and Bad of Life

THOUGHT FOR TODAY: Though the fig tree do not blossom, nor fruit be on the vines . . . yet I will rejoice in the LORD. . . . Habakkuk 3:17, 18

I live in a place where, during part of the year, refreshing breezes, singing birds, and green hillsides make life seem very beautiful.

At other times there is the beauty of snow. However, sometimes the snow must be shoveled, firewood must be gathered, and one must walk to church when the car won't start.

The God who makes gushing springs, sunshine, and flowers, also makes wind, rain, dirt, and cold weather. We can be certain that God will be with us in all circumstances, helping us to appreciate the good and giving strength to meet the bad.

PRAYER: Thank you, dear God, for letting us enjoy the beauties of nature and for being with us when life is not beautiful. Amen.

Phyllis Strong—Potlatch, Idaho

2 Corinthians 9:6–15   Cheerful Stewardship

THOUGHT FOR TODAY: Money is "coined personality."

Every one of us knows that money is a powerful factor in modern life. It is a necessity! It spells security, provides means of enjoyment, and is an instrument of service.

Dedicated Christians know that there are values worth more than money. A college president told students, "The length of your life is in the hands of God, the quality of your life is in your own hands." If we would live a life of quality we must consider what we do with money entrusted to us.

David Livingstone, a great missionary, said, "I will place no value on anything I have or may possess, except in its relation to the Kingdom of Christ." What a concept! Paul in 2 Corinthians 9:7 suggests, "God loves a cheerful giver." Examine your giving outlook. It's a privilege to share in advancing kingdom enterprises.

PRAYER: O God of the abundant life, teach me the stewardship way of joyful giving. Amen.   *Raymond M. Veh—Thiensville, Wisconsin*

Psalm 31:19–24   Returning God's Love

THOUGHT FOR TODAY: As God constantly demonstrates love to us, God also delights in our communications of love.

My son and his wife were quietly driving down the highway with their two-year-old wedged between them. Susan was just learning to talk and had never spoken more than two or three sentences. Suddenly she stood, grabbed her daddy around the neck and burst out, "I love you, Daddy." How her spontaneous "I love you" set her daddy's heart to dancing!

Our finite minds have difficulty realizing that the heart of our God is gladdened by our expressions of love. It is awesome but true that the Creator of the universe is touched with our words of adoration.

John referred to himself as the disciple whom Jesus loved. It was John's affection for Jesus that enabled John to receive Jesus' love.

PRAYER: God, help us to love you more and to be childlike enough to express that love. Amen.   *Marie Shropshire—Wichita Falls, Texas*

Hebrews 11:23–29   Invisible Realities

THOUGHT FOR TODAY: . . . he persevered because he saw him who is invisible. Hebrews 11:27 (New International Version)

In a time when male infants were to be destroyed, Hebrew slaves risked their lives and the security of their family to preserve an infant son. Even as we ponder Moses' miraculous deliverance, however, we may fail to translate adequately the real message of that story into our own lives. Jochebed and Amram, ordinary Jewish citizens with far fewer privileges than any of us enjoy, so loved God and Moses that they refused to allow their standards of conduct to be dictated by a totalitarian government.

Their courage produced a son who later chose to suffer hardship with God's people rather than enjoy the treasures of Egypt. Together they demonstrated "that the sufferings of this present time are not worthy to be compared with the glory which shall be revealed in us" (Romans 8:18, King James Version).

PRAYER: God, constantly remind us that the important realities of life are unseen and eternal. In Jesus' name. Amen.

Patricia Souder—Montrose, Pennsylvania

Ephesians 2:11–18; Matthew 5:9   More Than Armistice

THOUGHT FOR TODAY: . . . Peace is a precious gift that is not to be kept or hoarded but to be generously shared.

By act of Congress in 1954, Armistice Day became Veterans Day. On this day we are asked to honor those who serve and have served in the armed forces of the United States, with special remembrance of those who have given their lives in the service of their country. As meaningful as the change in name may be, we ought not lose entirely the significance of the term "armistice," which the dictionary defines as a stopping of warfare, preliminary to signing a peace treaty; a truce.

Sadly, the armistice of November 11, 1918, was broken. How fragile is peace on human terms! How different is the peace that is the gracious gift of God through our Lord Jesus Christ. More than armistice is that true peace, which is not merely a truce, but which brings complete reconciliation, replacing enmity with love, trust, and caring compassion.

PRAYER: Dear God of Peace, create within us an ever-increasing desire for your peace to share with all people everywhere. Amen.

Oliver E. Peterson—Lansdale, Pennsylvania

167

Ephesians 6:10–18   Christian Perseverance

THOUGHT FOR TODAY: Giving it another try is better than an alibi; but perseverance, through Christ, gives power to weakness.

It is told that Robert Bruce, one-time king of Scotland, had a moment of discouragement. He then observed a spider try over and over again to fasten a thread of its web. At last the spider succeeded, whereupon Bruce sprang up and went to the attack once more, and that time it ended in success.

Perseverance in the cause of Christ is a quality to be desired. It is good for each of us to determine what our foremost Christian talent is and to persevere in its development. It might be teaching, witnessing, praying for others.

Then, when the art of perseverance has polished up that foremost talent, let's develop that latent second talent.

PRAYER: Dear God, thank you for spiritual aspirations. Help us to fill our special niche in your plan. In Christ's name. Amen.

Edna Elsaser—Boonville, New York

Psalm 19:7–14   An Unseen Guest

THOUGHT FOR TODAY: May the words of my mouth and the meditation of my heart be pleasing in your sight. . . . Psalm 19:14 (New International Version)

One morning as I switched on the radio and began tuning in a favorite station, I suddenly heard distinctly familiar voices. Listening closely I realized my radio was receiving the early morning activity around my neighbor's breakfast table! Apparently a baby monitor located in her son's bedroom transmitted at a frequency that my own radio picked up. Imagine her surprise when I told her that she had entertained an unseen guest for breakfast that morning.

I, too, have an ever-present unseen guest in my home. But how easy it is to forget His presence. He promised, ". . . I am with you always, to the close of the age" (Matthew 28:20). Oh, how I need that reminder!

PRAYER: Lord, may what I do and say this day be reflective of Christ living in me. In Jesus' name. Amen.

Sally Ritter—Franklinville, New Jersey

Job 4:3–7   Facing Yourself

THOUGHT FOR TODAY: The individual who knows Jesus Christ becomes a clear thinker.

Christianity seeks to help people ready themselves by shoring them up on the inside, by making them adequate for any circumstances that may develop. Christianity helps people to stand up to life's problems. This is an essential function of preaching in this age.

Eliphaz the Temanite said to Job, "Your words have helped the tottering to stand, and you have strengthened weak hands" (Job 4:4, New American Standard). That is a dynamite statement! The text implies that we should stand up to our problems and overcome our weaknesses.

We stagger under the overwhelming pressures of our time. We have not learned, with all of our knowledge, to understand completely the human personality. But Christ still seeks to save the person who honestly asks, "Is it I?"

PRAYER: We thank you, God, for the great, yet simple truth that when Jesus dominates our lives, the shadow of gloom can never remain. Amen.

Jack Naff—Hood River, Oregon

2 Corinthians 12:1–10   Perfect Power in Weakness

THOUGHT FOR TODAY: Troubles can be transformed into triumphs.

Paul relates in today's Scripture an experience that he had had, speaking of his handicap as "a thorn in the flesh." It had come to him from Satan, but not without the consent and purpose of God. A thorn can be very painful and annoying. Paul, therefore, three times asked for deliverance that he might better serve God. Each time the answer was "My grace is sufficient for you, for my power is made perfect in weakness" (2 Corinthians 12:9).

With much grace and with complete confidence in the One to whom he had committed himself, Paul added the words "I will all the more gladly boast of my weaknesses that the power of Christ may rest upon me." With equal confidence and trust, we, too, may commit ourselves to the power of God to control every circumstance in which we find ourselves and thus to transform troubles into triumphs.

PRAYER: God, increase our trust in you even when we cannot see. In Jesus' name. Amen.   *Theodore E. Bubeck—Lakewood, New Jersey*

Psalm 121   Have Faith in God

THOUGHT FOR TODAY: [Jesus said] ". . . he who follows me will not walk in darkness. . . ." John 8:12

As I drove along a highway one morning, fog shrouded the way ahead, giving me a feeling of unease, for it was difficult to see clearly where I was going.

Often our lives are shrouded by the fogs of uncertainty. We feel afraid and alone. In our despair we fail to see the light of God's love shining through the darkness to assure us that we are neither forgotten nor forsaken. When we believe fully in God's goodness and power, the mists of our uncertainties will fade away and the path God wants us to take will be seen more clearly. When troubles come to us, we can always trust the One who said, "I am the way."

PRAYER: Help us to remember, God, that you are with us always. We have confidence in your sustaining power. Help us to walk without fear. In Jesus' name we pray. Amen.   *Gussie Casteel—Springfield, Missouri*

Romans 8:31–39   God at the Center

THOUGHT FOR TODAY: . . . in all things God works for good with those who love him, those whom he has called according to his purpose. Romans 8:28 *(Good News Bible)*

Marj had a rare disease that left her bedridden for a week, sometimes two, out of every four. Only after a number of miscarriages did she succeed in bearing a lovely daughter. No woman with her problem had ever had a second child. But after more miscarriages she did. Then, when the girls were one and three years old, her husband died.

Marj says that without her faith she could not have coped. Instead of retreating, she went out to meet life. She became a loyal and faithful part of her church. After the girls went to school, she spent her days visiting sick and elderly people, doing their errands, writing their letters if they were blind, transporting them in her old car that seemed to be held together only by her faith. Later, when the girls were in bed, she did her housework. She enjoyed life, because God was at the center.

PRAYER: God, sometimes I feel lonely and discouraged. Help me to be your person even then and to be on top of life. Amen.

Richard Lawton—Adelaide, Australia

Isaiah 55:2–6   Real Living

THOUGHT FOR TODAY: ". . . Come to me and you will have life!" Isaiah 55:3 *(Good News Bible)*

We humans are constantly seeking ways to improve life. We work hard to earn a living so that we can buy more things. Possessions have become a status symbol of our wealth. If we don't have the money, we'll buy on credit. What happens if and when we attain these possessions? Are we then satisfied? Only temporarily.

The fact is that our true happiness can never come from what we have. We will always have a void there. But God can fill that void. God is the only one who can give us life in all of its fullness. But we must choose to come to God if we want a taste of real honest-to-goodness living.

PRAYER: Our God, help me find my happiness in you and live life in all of its fullness. In Jesus' name. Amen.

Jeri Sweany—Annapolis, Maryland

1 Peter 3:12 God Hears All Prayers

THOUGHT FOR TODAY: For the eyes of the Lord are upon the righteous and his ears are open to their prayers. 1 Peter 3:12

Shortly after my Vietnamese-born wife accepted Christ as her Savior, I unexpectedly came upon her in prayer—her eyes closed and head bowed. When she finished, she looked up at me and said, "Honey, when I pray to God, I pray in Vietnamese. Will God hear and understand me?"

I explained that God reads our hearts, not our lips. But her question reminded me that we are all God's children and God judges and blesses us for our righteousness, not for the color of our skin, the shape of our eyes, or the language in which we pray.

PRAYER: Thank you, God, for an abundance of love to fill all those who seek it. Amen. *Ron Humphrey—Arlington, Virginia*

Luke 10:30–37 Justice and Mercy

THOUGHT FOR TODAY: . . . What doth the LORD require of thee, but to do justly, and to love mercy, and to walk humbly with thy God? Micah 6:8 (King James Version)

I see the outstretched hand of a naked child who begs for a crust of bread, and I wonder, "Where is mercy?"

I see the pious man gathering his robes about him, passing by on the other side and ignoring the distasteful scene of a suffering human being. Again I wonder, "Where is compassion?"

I see a rich man who has attained his wealth through trampling the poor and oppressing the less fortunate. I ponder, "Where is humility?"

I see the criminally insane person who is set free to frighten and threaten humanity. My heart cries out, "Where is justice?"

Justice and mercy are attributes of God. The only requirement made of those who love God is that they, as God's humble instruments, promote the cause of justice and mercy in the world.

PRAYER: God of justice and mercy, sharpen my awareness of injustice and cruelty in our world so that I may stand against them. In Jesus' name. Amen. *Shirley Myers—Zanesville, Ohio*

1 Peter 2:1–12   People Who "Go Bump" in the Day

THOUGHT FOR TODAY: Live such good lives among the pagans that, though they accuse you of doing wrong, they may see your good deeds and glorify God. . . . 1 Peter 2:12 (New International Version)

At a Rock and Pebble Show, one display caught my eye. Many ordinary-looking small rocks were placed in a container filled with a special fluid. Then, at a terrific rate of speed, the container turned and the rocks moved. When, finally, the rocks were taken out, they were shining bright. By bumping against each other, with the help of the liquid, they had brought out the best in each other.

In the New Testament, Christians are urged to put up with one another, help one another, and love one another. In everyday life we sometimes "bump" into each other. We are to use those times, with the aid of the Holy Spirit, to bring out the best in each other. By allowing God's love to flow through us to love difficult people, we become the people God redeemed us to be.

PRAYER: God, you have called us to be together as your people. Love through us everyone we meet today, for Jesus' sake. Amen.

William K. Webb—Clifton, New Jersey

Matthew 7:24–29   The Rock of God's Love

THOUGHT FOR TODAY: But for those who honor the LORD, his love lasts forever. . . . Psalm 103:17 *(Good News Bible)*

While walking along a river bed, I picked up a rock about the size and shape of an egg. It was so worn by the tons of water that must have passed over it that it felt smooth and satiny to my touch.

When rivers of troubled waters pass over us, sometimes we feel unworthy and alone. Then is when we need to remember that, in spite of outward appearances, we can depend on God's promises. The rock I found had all of its rough edges worn off, and it had attained a mellow sort of beauty. We, too, can find beauty in our lives if we remember that in spite of troubles and outward appearances, God's love is stronger than our troubled waters.

PRAYER: God, I need your love every hour. Help me when I am so troubled that I fail to remember your love is there. Amen.

Hazel Laughlin—Walla Walla, Washington

James 2:18–26   Believe and Do

THOUGHT FOR TODAY: Show me your faith apart from your works, and I by my works will show you my faith. James 2:18

The writer James scarcely wins a prize for popularity. Crusty and stern in his letter, he rebukes fellow Christians who "play up" to the wealthy and think of faith by itself as a virtue. Addressing a late first-century church that tended to make faith academic, James insists that believing and doing must stand together.

Crusty as he may sound, James makes a point crucial to life: *doing* must go with *believing*. Believing that forward motion keeps a bicycle in balance, we must get up on that bicycle and ride. Believing that our Lord journeyed from heaven to earth, we must at times make our journeys from safe to dangerous places. Believing in the ultimate kingdom, we must open ourselves to many peoples in our own diverse world.

PRAYER: Strengthen us, God, not only to believe but to do; not only to preach the Good News but to live it. In Jesus' name. Amen.

Hugh Dickinson—Lansdowne, Pennsylvania

173

Colossians 3:1–7   Real Thanks

THOUGHT FOR TODAY: . . . sing psalms and hymns and spiritual songs with thankfulness in your hearts to God. Colossians 3:16

We can't be really thankful for daily bread unless we have suffered hunger. We can't be really thankful for steady work and regular income unless we have been unemployed. America as a nation sits around food-laden Thanksgiving Day tables and proves only that we are a nation of gluttons.

The Colossian Christians knew the peace and freedom of being set free from the enslavement of earthly things. They were encouraged to express their feelings in songs and praise and thanksgiving to God. If we stop and count our blessings, naming each one specifically, we too will be moved to songs and praise and thanks to the Lord. A thankful, singing heart gives joy to daily living.

PRAYER: Help me to see how you are in everything that happens in my life. I praise and thank you! In Jesus' name. Amen.

Walter B. Wakeman—Rockland, Maine

Hebrews 11:1–2; 13:1–6 God's Limits

THOUGHT FOR TODAY: God is the one in complete control of the future.

After a day of playing miniature golf, riding go-karts, and hiking through the woods, our eleven-year-old son began asking questions about the future. Why were people in other countries fighting? Would those wars eventually come to our country? Although our son didn't seem upset, still my husband wanted to ease his young mind.

"Remember the go-karts today?" he asked, getting a responsive nod. "For our own good, the owner put limiters on them so they'd go only a certain speed. For our own good, God puts limiters on our knowing the future. God lets us know enough to prepare adequately and yet not enough to control it. It's our faith in God and God's controls that will help us in the future."

PRAYER: Dear God, as an act of faith, we give you our lives and futures so that your will may be done. In Jesus' name. Amen.

Carol Hegberg—DeKalb, Illinois

Colossians 3:1–4 Higher Things

THOUGHT FOR TODAY: I press on toward the goal for the prize of the upward call of God in Christ Jesus. Phillippians 3:14

Outside our patio doors, suspended from the eaves of the house, a lovely basket of fuchsia cascades pink and purple beauty. Far above the drab concrete floor, often wet and streaked with the slimy trails of garden slugs, the basket of color lifts one's soul toward the Creator of all inspiring things.

On the back fence, beyond the green lawn, an ambitious rose vine has sent one of its longest branches up through the center of a ten-foot lilac bush, exulting at the top of the bush in a striking tiara of crimson bloom.

Seeking higher things is also a motivating spring within our human natures. When we are rightly related to our Creator, we experience the upward promptings of the Spirit.

PRAYER: God of our lives, help us to take time to feed our souls on the nourishment your Spirit so generously supplies and to keep on the upward climb, ever seeking your beckoning will. Amen.

Kenneth C. Hendricks—Salem, Oregon

Isaiah 40:3–5, 26–31 — Expanded Awareness

THOUGHT FOR TODAY: "The glory of the Lord will be seen by all. . . ." Isaiah 40:5 *(The Living Bible)*

I moved from Pennsylvania to Arizona last year. One change this move provided is a better view of the sky. I love the expansive sky of the Southwest and all that it symbolizes.

The God of all that is has called us to look beyond our present horizons to expanded awareness and deepened sensitivity, to greater aliveness and deeper peace, and much more.

We have the potential of expanding our sensitivity for human need and our awareness of God's loving activity in and through us. The resources of life are greater than the problems we encounter.

God knows how much courage it takes to go out to the unknown, to risk where we have not been, to stretch beyond the familiar. That's why Jesus came to show us the way. May your celebration of Advent—the coming of Christ—lead you to expanded awareness of God's love and a larger vision of opportunities before you.

PRAYER: O loving God, expand our awareness so that each time we see the sky we'll be reminded of your great love through Christ. Amen.

Paul W. Strickland—Prescott, Arizona   175

Genesis 1:26–31 — All in God's Time

THOUGHT FOR TODAY: "Do not be anxious for tomorrow; for tomorrow will care for itself." Matthew 6:34a (New American Standard Bible)

The great oak did not grow in one instant. God did not make the world in one day. Our own observation reveals that God is still refining both, even giving us opportunity to help.

If God and nature patiently take one moment or day at a time to reach the ultimate in their plan or potential, wouldn't it be well for me to develop a more relaxed attitude?

I will try taking one step at a time in my daily life and my work, trusting that gradually and eventually I will accomplish all that I should.

PRAYER: Dear God, Increase my observation and understanding of your ways. In Jesus' name.

Lois Berger Swartz—Watsontown, Pennsylvania

John 11:21–27 Rebirth

THOUGHT FOR TODAY: God communicates with us to strengthen our belief in the promise of everlasting life by Jesus Christ.

A friend gave me a plant which many call the "prayer plant." She said, "It's not doing very well with me. See if you'll have better luck with it." For quite a while the plant flourished. Then it became pale and withered and died. I forgot about the plant as other things needed my attention.

Several days later, I was about to dispose of the dead prayer plant when I was astounded to see a profusion of young green shoots! In a surprisingly short time, I had a more beautiful plant than I had before!

This rebirth of my prayer plant was, to me, a miracle! I firmly believed that God, in his great love, was reminding me of Jesus' promise of the resurrection. I was filled with hope, faith, and joy!

PRAYER: Our God, thank you for your blessings and for the promise of eternal life by your Son, our Savior. Amen.

Margaret Heggan—Philadelphia, Pennsylvania

Hebrews 8:8–12 God's Forgiveness Is Real

THOUGHT FOR TODAY: We can accept ourselves as acceptable because God in Christ has accepted us.

There was, and may still be somewhere, a little old lady harried and continually distraught. She fretted herself about sin and about having committed sins that had slipped out of sight under the bed of years or in some dark corner of her soul, all unconfessed. She disturbed her friend and neighbor to distraction about it. One morning her friend came to her house and said, "Hattie, I came today on purpose to tell you God ain't got nothing against you." It was, I think, E. Stanley Jones who said, "God buries our sins in the sea of His forgetfulness and puts up a sign, 'No Fishing Here.' "

PRAYER: Lord, help us grasp that Jesus has burst upon our lives with the excitement of showing that you have nothing against us. Amen.

Frank Harris—Cedar Falls, Iowa

DECEMBER

Mark 13:33–37   Coming, Ready or Not!

THOUGHT FOR TODAY: "And what I say to you I say to all: Watch." Mark 13:37

The season of Advent is a time of preparation for the observance of Jesus' birth. It reminds us that all truly worthwhile events are those that call for us to get ready. Company is coming; get ready. A special anniversary will soon be here; get ready. It's time to move into that new home; get ready.

Advent allows us to get ready for Christmas, the coming of Jesus to this earth as a baby. But he's coming, ready or not. Some were not ready when Jesus came as a baby; but he came, ready or not.

I want to be ready for that happy day so that "Merry Christmas" will not be just words but a deeply felt experience with the living Christ.

PRAYER: Make us ready to meet the Lord in a very special way in this season of joy. In his name we pray. Amen.

E. Harris Paulson—North Canton, Ohio

Matthew 18:1–5   A Little Child Shall Lead

THOUGHT FOR TODAY: . . . that Christ may dwell in your hearts through faith. . . . Ephesians 3:17

I was busily engaged in helping my four-year-old grandniece, Heather, with her dishes following one of her "tea parties." She was telling me of the real birthday cake she and her mother had made—a very special one.

When I asked Heather whose birthday it was, she replied, "Jesus'." And when I asked her if we were going to have a party, she assured me we were. Then she became very serious and thoughtful and finally asked, "How Him get down here?" I assured her that Jesus is here all the time and that we just don't exactly see him. At this point she placed her hand over her heart and said, "Him live in our hearts."

What a highlight of that week! Certainly "a little child shall lead."

PRAYER: Thank you, Lord, for the witness of a little child and for the privilege of having Jesus living within us. Amen.

June E. Skeels—Green Lake, Wisconsin

Psalm 100   Life's Extras

THOUGHT FOR TODAY: We do not live by bread alone. We're thankful too for the beauty of the rose, the song of the lark, and much more.

At the close of the children's sermon that Sunday before Thanksgiving Day, the children were asked to mention one thing for which they were particularly thankful. One youngster responded: "I'm glad for the things I have that I don't really have to have."

The child had learned early in life to be thankful not only for the material and spiritual things which enrich our lives, but for the many lovely "extras" which we receive from the hands of God. Such things as paintings, poetry, books, the laughter of children at play, the love of a mother for her child, and a friend for his friend.

PRAYER: As we arise each morning, dear Lord, give us an appreciation of the many "extras" you send our way. In Jesus' name. Amen.

Erma Fajen MacFarlane—Columbia, Missouri

Luke 2:8–11   Wonder

THOUGHT FOR TODAY: . . . and they were filled with fear. Luke 2:9

Who knows what the shepherds saw, heard, felt? What reality is shrouded in the words "the glory of the Lord shone around them"? This much is certain: there was the overwhelming sense of confrontation with the divine. God speaks. Humans hear. Extraordinary! There was the element of surprise, the element of mystery, the element of speechless awe. Suddenly there was the profound awareness of being addressed by the almighty and ineffable God. In the midst of the mundane and the routine, God manifests himself.

Christmas means that suddenly, dramatically, decisively God breaks into the circle of our human reality, the divine "tour de force." The only appropriate response is awe—awe mixed with joy, gratitude, and surrender.

Sing "While Shepherds Watched Their Flocks by Night."

PRAYER: God, restore a sense of awe to our Christmas worship. In Jesus' name. Amen.   *Donald D. Morris—Montclair, New Jersey*

Luke 9:18–27   Who Is He?

THOUGHT FOR TODAY: "Who do you say that I am?" And Peter answered, "The Christ of God." Luke 9:20

To the first Jewish Christians Jesus was the Messiah. Calvinism emphasized the stern Lord of the Last Judgment. In art Jesus has been depicted as a fat baby in the arms of a benign Madonna. Bonhoeffer called him "the man for others." In the 1960s Jesus was the "suffering servant."

Who is Jesus for the 1980s? In the passage for today Peter blurted out, "The Christ of God." The *Good News Bible* translates, "You are God's Messiah." J.B. Phillips says, "God's Christ."

Paul answered the question this way: "Christ Jesus was in the form of God . . . who emptied himself, taking the form of a servant." John called him "The light of the world," "the bread of life," "the way, the truth, and the life."

Paul Tillich called Jesus "the New Being" who brings reconciliation, re-union and resurrection.

PRAYER: God, give us courage to ask the hard question: "Who is Christ for me?" In Christ's name we pray. Amen.

Richard L. Keach—Hartford, Connecticut

179

John 1:1–5   Christmas—Glitter or Glow?

THOUGHT FOR TODAY: Christmas is more than a one-time flash; it is a continuing light.

Our granddaughter had been sitting at the dining room table using paste and sprinkling glitter on the pictures that Grandma had cut out for her. Although her "mess" was cleaned up later, here and there brightly colored specks were occasionally seen for months later.

Christmas should be like these flecks of sparkling glitter and not one big blazing flash here one day and gone the next. The light of the world came into the world on Christmas Day—to stay! Because of our faith in Him, our lives have been given a glitter and a glow. And it will shine in the strangest places if we let it! The light may be surrounded by darkness, but the darkness cannot extinguish it.

PRAYER: Dear God, this Christmas season let your light shine forth from our hearts that others might see and believe also. In Jesus' name. Amen.   *Richard K. Mercer, Jr.—Titusville, Pennsylvania*

Matthew 28:16–20   "Always with You"

THOUGHT FOR TODAY: Fear thou not; for I am with thee. . . . Isaiah 41:10 (King James Version)

Moses was justifiably fearful, wondering whether he was being sent on an unwieldy task alone, and so he prayed: "If thy presence go not with me, carry us not up hence" (Exodus 33:15, KJV). Jeremiah responded in a similar manner when God called him: "I can't do it alone; I'm but a child. Call someone else."

To the eleven whom Jesus sent forth he gave this familiar promise: ". . . and, lo, I am with you alway, even unto the end of the world" (Matthew 28:20, KJV). In other words: "You need not walk alone."
PRAYER: God, help us to realize that you are always with us so that we need never feel alone. In Jesus' name. Amen.

Theodore E. Bubeck—Lakewood, New Jersey

Luke 2:8–14   The Field of the Shepherds

THOUGHT FOR TODAY: Without the life-giving Spirit of God, external worship is meaningless.

And in that region there were shepherds out in the field, keeping watch over their flock by night" (Luke 2:8). So begins the announcement to the shepherds of the birth of our Savior. What field? Where? Some time ago, the Greek Orthodox Church said they found the exact field where the shepherds received their announcement! It was on property held sacred by the church! Archbishop Constantine told how excavators had discovered the ruins of a church dating back to the fifth century, one mile east of Bethlehem. Nearby are two pieces of land that both the Protestants and Catholics revere. All three are called shepherds' fields. So the shepherds must have been out on three different fields!

Jesus told the woman of Samaria, whom he met by the well, that the true worship of God was in spirit and truth, and that the place was incidental. For with the incarnation, God coming in the flesh of Jesus Christ, there came a whole new dimension to worship. God was no longer tied down to a physical place, a location, a nation, a field! He was now available to all persons everywhere—anywhere!
PRAYER: Thank you, Jesus, that to those who will let you be born in their hearts, there will be a well of water springing up into everlasting life. Amen.   *Richard K. Mercer, Jr.—Titusville, Pennsylvania*

Matthew 1:18–25   Good News in a Baby

THOUGHT FOR TODAY: ". . . I bring you good news of a great joy which will come to all the people." Luke 2:10

The poets have said that every birth of a child is proof that God is not yet discouraged with humans.

One of my life's greatest joys was to be with Carol when our son, Nathan, was born. Those moments of birth were filled with great excitement, a deep sense of wonder at the beauty and mystery of creation, the joy of love fulfilled, and thanksgiving for this new life given to us.

This Christmas will again have new meaning as we remember Mary and Joseph as the Christ child is born. Let the birth of the baby Jesus be moments of great excitement filled with a deep sense of wonder, great joy for God's love, and thanksgiving for the new life he brings.

PRAYER: God, as we read and hear the Christmas story again this year, help us to hear the Good News of your love. In Christ's name we pray. Amen.   *Gary W. Wagner—Green Lake, Wisconsin*

Matthew 6:25–34   He Knows

THOUGHT FOR TODAY: Let him have all your worries and cares, for he is always thinking about you and watching everything that concerns you. 1 Peter 5:7 *(The Living Bible)*

I had been feeling really discouraged and anxious about our financial situation. After a period of unemployment, we were getting deeper in debt each month. We just recently had had to replace a major appliance; our car needed extensive repair work; we had high medical expenses; our charge accounts were near their credit ceilings; and our savings were low.

Then one afternoon after coming home from the women's circle I was leading at church, I found an envelope in our mailbox with the above verse from First Peter printed on it. As I opened the envelope, I found to my amazement that it contained $150. Truly the Lord did know our needs and proved how much he cares by prompting one of his people to share with us. I was overwhelmed and humbled, as well as determined to pass along God's love by sharing with others whose needs are even greater than ours.

PRAYER: Thank you, Lord, that you care about my needs. Let this knowledge free me to respond to the needs of others. Amen.

Marlene Bagnull—Drexel Hill, Pennsylvania

Colossians 1:15–20   Christ Universal

THOUGHT FOR TODAY: ". . . good news of a great joy which will come to all the people. . . ." Luke 2:10

The gospel, the redemptive purpose of God in the shape of a human life, is, according to our New Testament, the property of everyone who lives and breathes. It is a gospel for "all the people."

How so? The New Testament does not leave the question unaddressed. That which was revealed within the boundaries of a particular human life is precisely the universal Spirit, the Spirit that creates and sustains, bears upon and influences all life. There is no one, be he or she ever so remote from Christendom, for whom Christmas is not the decisive event of history.

Sing "O Come, All Ye Faithful."

PRAYER: Omnipresent God, thank you for including all of humanity in your redemptive will. In Jesus' name. Amen.

Donald D. Morris—Montclair, New Jersey

Matthew 2:1–12   Travelers from Afar

THOUGHT FOR TODAY: We come by different roads to seek the Savior, and all the while he has been waiting for us to come.

What a wild ride the wise men had, at least as it is described by T. S. Eliot, who wrote a poem which attempts to scrape off the hard veneer of romanticism covering the journey of the Eastern kings seeking Jesus!

In the poem, an aged member of the caravan recalls some of the hardships of the trip. It was quite unpleasant. The doubts of the worth of their mission haunted them with "voices singing in our ears, saying that this was all folly." But finally they found the Christ child, and their whole journey was blessed!

We come by different roads to seek the Savior, and all the while he has been waiting for us to come! Sometimes the road is one of light and music, but most often it is difficult, rugged, and soul shattering. But when we have found him, we have found the answer to life itself. It has been worth the journey!

PRAYER: Lord, keep reminding us that the difficult journey we often must travel is worth it when it leads to thee. For Jesus' sake. Amen.

Richard K. Mercer, Jr.—Titusville, Pennsylvania

Matthew 2:16–18   The Judean Children

THOUGHT FOR TODAY: They died when he was born; we live because he died. By faith everybody could.

We often hear it said that Christmas is for children. I have heard, too, that Sunday church school is for children, intimating that it is not for adults. Again, I've heard persons say they don't mind if their wives take the children to church but . . . Yes, they mean it's not for grown men.

I well remember one of my granddaughters kneeling before a manger scene on our front porch. Recently her very young son did about the same at his grandmother's house. Yes, Christmas is for children.

Matthew told of Judean children who never heard of the birth of the Messiah. Some expositors have made it seem that was less of a concern than we used to think of it, because really there were not so many of them, fifty maybe! But, one or a million, they were dead. Christmas *is* for children—and for *you* and for *me!*

PRAYER: Lord Jesus, we want to keep it that way. May your Spirit enable us to do so! In your name we pray. Amen.

E. James Cain—Oroville, California

183

2 Corinthians 9:11–15   Left Out

THOUGHT FOR TODAY: Thanks be unto God for his unspeakable gift. 2 Corinthians 9:15 (King James Version)

When Everett was only five years old he attended a church Christmas party. Under the tree lay many gifts. Each child was invited to come up and take one present. When shy little Everett got to the tree, no gifts were left. He didn't cry, but he had trouble blinking back the tears. Everett never, ever, forgot that disappointment!

Years later, as Everett attended church and heard the gospel message, it was again Christmas, and Everett's heart was stirred as he finally realized that *Jesus* was God's unspeakable gift to *him!* Now he knew that he had *not* been left out. God had given him the most priceless gift of all and had saved it for the time when he was ready to accept it.

Never again did Everett resent that Christmas long ago.

PRAYER: Thank you God, for your unspeakable gift, your son, Jesus. In his name. Amen.   *Mary Lou Klingler—Phoenix, Arizona*

Matthew 25:35–40 God Speaks

THOUGHT FOR TODAY: God loveth a cheerful giver.

A young minister's wife answered the door to greet an early morning caller, a member of their church. The member handed her two dollars, saying, "Mother asked me to bring you this." With tears in her eyes, the minister's wife asked, "How did she know this was needed?" The member stated that her mother had a feeling that help was needed; so she gathered up some of her hens and sold them to the peddler.

Just that morning the minister and his wife had discussed a need that must be met that day, not knowing that, perhaps while they were speaking, God had spoken to a church member.

The member did not have many of this world's goods, but she felt in her heart another's need and so was willing to share what she had.

Such acts not only meet a need but also bring joy in sharing as in receiving, strengthening the hearts and lives of others.

PRAYER: We praise thee, God, for thy spirit manifest in so many saints who have walked this earth, who have shared acts of love. Amen.

Matilda Pyle—Largo, Florida

1 Peter 2:4–8 Our Cornerstone

THOUGHT FOR TODAY: The Lord is the foundation of my life and its cornerstone.

Years ago I watched workmen quarry limestone near Bedford, Indiana, for use in the RCA Building in New York City. Inspectors at the site painstakingly checked each stone to be sure that it was cut exactly right. If it wasn't, the stone was rejected.

Remembering those strict requirements for building stone, I have often wondered about 1 Peter 2:7, "To you therefore who believe, he is precious, but for those who do not believe, 'The very stone which the builders rejected has become the head of the corner.' "

Too often we let our human, sophisticated standards overpower God's way. Only through faith can we believe that a rejected stone has become the head of the corner.

PRAYER: O God, we thank you that what we can't understand in the Bible, we can believe in faith. In Jesus' name. Amen.

R. H. Windbigler—Olathe, Kansas

John 1:1–5   Amid Christmas Cookies

THOUGHT FOR TODAY: The light shines in the darkness, and the darkness has not overcome it. John 1:5

On a dark December evening I was hurriedly slipping fresh-baked cookies off a cookie sheet. I was feeling the Christmas rush of things to do. Then I noticed a folded piece of paper on the table. I began reading what our ten-year-old daughter Karen had written: "Christmas is a time of sharing. Presents make others happy and you at the same time. But Christmas is not just presents and trees and decorations; it celebrates Christ's birth. There once was a man named Joseph and a woman named Mary. When they got to Bethlehem, they found no rooms anywhere. In a manger place their Son Jesus was born to tell the Good News of God. As Son of God he created many miracles and one day rose from the dead. The celebration of this goes on."

PRAYER: Dear God, fill us with your love and peace at Christmas in a celebration that goes on and on. Amen.

Charlotte and Karen Adelsperger—Prairie Village, Kansas

Luke 2:1–7   Humility

THOUGHT FOR TODAY: And she gave birth to her first-born son and wrapped him in swaddling cloths, and laid him in a manger. . . . Luke 2:7

What circumstances should surround the birth of a king? What is proper and acceptable for a divine emissary? The Magi, so we are informed later in our story (Matthew 2:2), went to Jerusalem inquiring, " 'Where is he who has been born king of the Jews?' " Of course, kings are born in the palaces of kings. The fact is, however, that—given an overview of his life, given the spiritual dimension of the kingdom that he proclaimed, and given the prominent place in that kingdom accorded the poor—the stable was entirely commensurate with the birth of Jesus. It was right and good.

The correspondence of the birth of Jesus to the manner in which it is celebrated in an opulent society is worth pondering. A question also arises from this consideration: Is there no irony in our manner of celebrating the birth of one who espoused poverty and simplicity?

PRAYER: Loving God, teach us the meaning of our Lord's beatitude: "Blessed are the poor in spirit. . . ." Amen.

Donald D. Morris—Montclair, New Jersey

Matthew 1:18–25 Let's Not Forget the Reason

THOUGHT FOR TODAY:". . . she will have a Son, and you shall name him Jesus . . . for he will save his people from their sins." Matthew 1:21 *(The Living Bible)*

When Christmas comes around, most of us are busy baking cookies, shopping, and wrapping presents. However, we often forget what Christmas is all about.

There was a girl in our kindergarten department who didn't forget though. When I asked her what she was going to do on Christmas morning, she said, "Before I wake up my mommy, I'm going to sing 'Happy Birthday' to Jesus." She had the real "Christmas spirit."

Christmas is truly a happy time; however, we must not forget that it is the Lord's birthday. Jesus was born so that he could teach the world about God and then die to save the world from sin. So this Christmas, before we open our gifts, let's not forget to thank God for the gift he gave us.

PRAYER: Dear Lord, help us to remember that Christmas is Jesus' birthday. Amen. *Bill Wright—San Jose, California*

186

Luke 2:8–15 God's Great Gift

THOUGHT FOR TODAY: "For to you is born this day in the city of David a Savior, who is Christ the Lord." Luke 2:11

To you is born a Savior. To whom? The news of the birth of the Savior did not come to the emperor in Rome, nor to Herod in Jerusalem, nor to the religious priests and scribes, nor to those who believed they were righteous. It was to the shepherds in the fields that the news was given of a Savior who was born.

Who are the shepherds? They represent the small and insignificant people who have little hope for a better life. They represent the poor and oppressed peoples of the world who have been exploited by the rich and powerful. They represent the humble, the patient, and the obedient of God's people.

To them, to all people comes the message of hope: "You have a Savior who is Christ the Lord." In him you will find life. In him there is hope.

PRAYER: Dear God, thank you for loving us by giving us the greatest gift you can, your Son Jesus. Amen.

Val J. Sauer, Jr.—Watertown, South Dakota

Luke 2:22–35   Vision

THOUGHT FOR TODAY: ". . . mine eyes have seen thy salvation. . . ." Luke 2:30

An interesting sidelight of the Christmas story is the meeting of Joseph, Mary, and the Child with the old Jewish mystic, Simeon. Simeon's prayer, known as the "Nunc Dimittis," has come down to us as one of the church's most beautiful liturgical expressions.

Little is known of Simeon. Luke pictures an obscure and insignificant old man frequenting the temple precincts, sustained and invigorated by a vision and a hope. Whatever it was precisely, it kept him alive beyond threescore and ten years. Simeon was a man who trusted and followed his intuition. Thus, at the promptings of the Spirit, he made his way into the temple at the precise point at which, according to Jewish prescription, the child Jesus was being formally presented to the Lord. This was his moment! How did he know? He just knew. In the shape—strange sight!—of a peasant woman's child he beheld the salvation of Israel and humanity. Without this vision there can be no Christmas.

PRAYER: Lord, you who are the Spirit and can be known only in spiritual communion, help us to see what Simeon beheld! Amen.

Donald D. Morris—Montclair, New Jersey   *187*

Matthew 1:18–25   God the Neighbor

THOUGHT FOR TODAY: ". . . his name shall be called Emmanuel" (which means, God with us). Matthew 1:23

In any situation of personal difficulty, particularly when difficulty degenerates into desperation, few words are quite so consoling as "I am with you." By virtue of this sentiment, filled with compassion and courage, humans identify themselves as "neighbor." "Neighbor" denotes the posture of "standing with." It means the determination to act redemptively on behalf of "the other person," even when the other person is "the enemy."

Jesus is the declaration of God's eternal determination to be with and for humanity. In Christ, God is manifested as humanity's neighbor.

PRAYER: Compassionate Lord, grant that we may be unto others as you are to us and all humanity. Amen.

Donald D. Morris—Montclair, New Jersey

Romans 1:1–6   Spiritual Origin

THOUGHT FOR TODAY: ". . . for that which is conceived in her is of the Holy Spirit. . . ." Matthew 1:20

Conceived by the Holy Spirit, Born of the Virgin Mary. . . ." Thus reads the Apostles' Creed. Let it be said that the significance of the church's doctrine of the virgin birth lies not in the assertion of a biological miracle. The scientific question of "how" is no concern of faith. Rather, the virgin birth is a testimony to the spiritual origin and destiny of the One whom the church recognizes as uniquely "Son of God." In other words, the church contends by virtue of this ancient doctrine that the phenomenon "Jesus Christ" cannot be explained in terms of human processes.

Christmas, in brief, is the celebration of One who, from the beginning and through all his days, was uniquely a child of the Spirit.

PRAYER: Dear God, make us aware of and responsive to the Spirit by which Jesus lived. Amen.   *Donald D. Morris—Montclair, New Jersey*

Philippians 2:5–11   God the Servant

THOUGHT FOR TODAY: . . . taking the form of a servant, being born in the likeness of men. Philippians 2:7

Jesus went unrecognized as the Lord's Messiah because humans could not conceive of God's deliverer in terms of—lo and behold—an eccentric, itinerant rabbi (known familiarly as "the carpenter's son"). It was the paradox of divine grace over which reason and expectation stumbled. The sovereign God of the universe, the creator and judge of humanity, does not bow down to the level of a manger and a cross. Theology doesn't permit it! "Humans serve God—God doesn't serve humans"; thus speaks a sane and proper dogmatics.

Alas! Christmas is the "foolish" celebration of just this "foolishness." Consider *this* Christmas text: "For the foolishness of God is wiser than men, and the weakness of God is stronger than men" (1 Corinthians 1:25).

PRAYER: Gracious God, thank you for teaching us that the One who is the servant of all is the greatest of all. Amen.

Donald D. Morris—Montclair, New Jersey

Luke 2:8–15 When God Comes Near

THOUGHT FOR TODAY: "And this will be a sign for you: you will find a babe wrapped in swaddling cloths and lying in a manger." Luke 2:12

What was the sign given signifying God's redeeming purpose for mankind? Was it some earth-shattering event? Was it the crowning of a new king? Was it the massing of armies or the uprising of whole nations? No! What the shepherds heard was this: "You will find a babe wrapped in swaddling cloths and lying in a manger."

The mighty God came to humankind in the weakness of flesh. In the life of Jesus, men and women, for the first time, could really see what God could mean to them. In the weakness of flesh, God redeemed humankind through Jesus Christ. And to "all who received him, who believed in his name, he gave power to become children of God" (John 1:12).

Your faith may be small, but God will use it. Trust God in little things, and you will see God's power in great events.

PRAYER: Thank you, God, for coming to us as we are, for meeting our needs, and in Jesus Christ, for making us your children. Amen.

Val J. Sauer, Jr.—Watertown, South Dakota

John 1:1–10 Light and Darkness

THOUGHT FOR TODAY: The true light that enlightens every man was coming into the world. John 1:9

Perhaps you have had the experience, as I have, of being temporarily in a situation of total darkness. Everything is pitch-black! Alone and insecure, one stands frozen in fear of the unseen. Few experiences can with such devastating rapidity shatter one's sense of equilibrium. In such a predicament the dim flicker of a candle in the distance means liberation! Light conquers the darkness. One's sight, made ineffective by the darkness, recovers its power of perspective.

Christmas is the celebration of light—the light of the presence of God that burns incessantly in the human breast. It is, moreover, preeminently the celebration of a human life in which this mysterious divine light showed through in unparalleled brilliance.

PRAYER: God of light, thank you for not leaving us in the darkness. Through Jesus Christ our Lord. Amen.

Donald D. Morris—Montclair, New Jersey

Matthew 4:18–22   The Sound of Command

THOUGHT FOR TODAY: Listen for a joyful noise!

It is recorded in Isaiah that God whistled. Why should that surprise me? Yet the thought of God whistling never occurred to me. However, Scripture is full of surprises. What delight to think of the sovereign One whistling. It makes me think of the song "Whistle While You Work." I wonder, did God whistle while creating, almost absentmindedly fluting as the stars were flung into space and the land was formed? When God said, "That's good," did a whistle escape in sheer pleasure? Then as humankind began to separate from God's sovereignty, was there a whistle of despair? Isaiah 5:26 tells us, "He whistles for those at the ends of the earth . . . they come swiftly and speedily" (New International Version).

God calls in unique ways. Are we listening?

PRAYER: God of the universe, thank you for revealing another dimension of your being. Empower us to live daily in response to your commands. In the name of Christ the incarnate One, amen.

Grace T. Lawrence—Mechanicsburg, Pennsylvania

2 Timothy 1:7–14   Emotional Wholeness

THOUGHT FOR TODAY: . . . for God did not give us a spirit of timidity. . . . 2 Timothy 1:7

We grow increasingly aware of the hectic pace at which we are called upon to live. Frustration is a national trait as we look on a world that is hungry, unjust, and undisciplined. How do we exhibit a spirit of peace in the face of so much unrest?

Our peace, of course, is not based on the world at rest or in its serenity. Our peace, our calmness, our emotional stability come from knowing a Savior who will keep those things which we have entrusted to him until the day when we claim them in true peace in his presence. We believe this, not in order to escape from the urnest of the world, but that we might face it and not be overcome. For "greater is he that is in you, than he that is in the world" (1 John 4:4, KJV).

PRAYER: As there is calmness in the eye of the storm, Lord, may we find refuge in the center of your love and promises as the storm swirls around us. Amen. *Frank Koshak—Prairie Village, Kansas*

Psalm 42   A Brook in Our Town

THOUGHT FOR TODAY: The brook would lose its song if we removed the rocks.

Through the center of our town runs a small stream that practically no one sees. It has been carefully channeled and neatly engineered so that it interferes with no one. Yet only two hundred yards upstream, the brook is a delightful scenic and bubbling cascade as it makes its way through a wooded section with wild flowers growing on its banks.

The brook reminds me, in this contrast, that all of our planning, all of our strategizing, all of our human engineering can make life safer and more orderly, but usually at the expense of beauty, excitement, and wonder. Sometimes it is good to risk a few rocks in the course of our living. It hurts a little, but the song is so much better and the scenery so much more pleasant!

PRAYER: O God, increase our appreciation of life as we bump over the rocks in the stream. Amen.   *John H. Minott—Chelmsford, Massachusetts*

1 Timothy 6:18–19   Foundations

THOUGHT FOR TODAY: "He shall be to you a restorer of life. . . ." Ruth 4:15

Some soils can crack your foundation," the radio announcer warned. The wry humor of this isolated statement, caught in passing, soon faded as the words took on a deeper meaning.

Who doesn't know someone suffering through the cracked foundation of a divorce? No one could know when the relationship began that the chemistry—the soil—was faulty.

Parents experience unsettled foundations when somehow they lose contact with a son or daughter. Underlying pressures, built up over a period of years, cause a hairline crack to become a major rift.

Some soils can crack your foundation, it's true; but we need not panic. The Master Builder maintains an open "prayer line" twenty-four hours a day.

PRAYER: Our God, we thank you for your loving support daily as well as in times of great stress. Amen.   *Mary A. Magers—Portland, Oregon*

Isaiah 40:27–31   Faith Renewed

THOUGHT FOR TODAY: Even when we are too weak to have any faith left, he remains faithful to us and will help us . . . he will always carry out his promises to us. 2 Timothy 2:13 *(The Living Bible)*

My daughter had been hospitalized for minor surgery, but the operation hadn't gone well. I was exhausted from the emotional strain and from running back and forth to the hospital while still caring for two little ones at home. I felt that the reservoir of my faith was drained and dry.

"Lord, please help me," I prayed. I opened my Bible and felt drawn to the above verse from Second Timothy. As I reflected on times in the past when God had helped me through difficult situations, I experienced his presence encouraging and enveloping me. His promises are not dependent on my feelings; they are beautiful, life-changing facts.

PRAYER: Forgive us, Lord, when we forget how very real and near you are. Thank you that even then you do not leave us alone. Amen.

Marlene Bagnull—Drexel Hill, Pennsylvania